LEARNING THROUGH

Junk materials

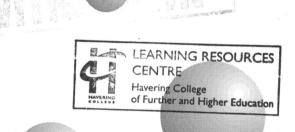

BARBARA J LEACH

Published by Scholastic Ltd,
Villiers House,
Clarendon Avenue,
Leamington Spa,
Warwickshire CV32 5PR
Text © Barbara J Leach
© 1997 Scholastic Ltd
2 3 4 5 6 7 8 9 0 8 9 0 1 2 3 4 5 6

Author
Barbara J Leach

Editor
Jane Bishop

Assistant editor
Libby Russell

Series designer
Lynne Joesbury

Designer
Rachel Warner

Illustrations
Claire Boyce

Cover photograph
Fiona Pragoff

The ideas in this book are based on an original proposal by Lynne Burgess, who
sadly died before she was able to write the book.

Designed using Aldus Pagemaker
Printed in Great Britain

British Library Cataloguing-in-Publication Data
A catalogue record for this book is available from the British Library.

ISBN 0-590-53715-6

CONTENTS

CHAPTER 4: KNOWLEDGE AND UNDERSTANDING OF THE WORLD

CHAPTER 5: PHYSICAL DEVELOPMENT

CHAPTER 6: CREATIVE DEVELOPMENT

PHOTOCOPIABLES

INTRODUCTION

Exploring the material

Junk materials can be the source of inspiration for a multitude of imaginative models – from trains to teddy bears; dragons to dominoes. They can also provide countless opportunities for sorting, classifying and measuring activities which are so vital in a young child's development. Moreover, the very act of re-using waste materials in a thoughtful way is a valuable lesson itself in this disposable age.

Every day there are opportunities to salvage packaging and other items which would otherwise be consigned to the dustbin (newspapers, envelopes, breakfast cereal boxes, egg cartons, kitchen roll tubes) which can form the basis of an excellent collection of materials to support learning across the whole curriculum. In fact, young children find junk materials so fascinating that they will often become so involved in the act of searching through the materials that they forget why they started looking in the first place!

Provide plenty of opportunities for the children to explore the materials before expecting them to settle down to more structured activities. With very young children, it is also a good idea to limit the range of materials available sometimes, in order to ensure that they concentrate on the set task rather than the junk itself.

Learning through play

Play is how children learn about themselves and the world around them. They explore and investigate, hypothesise and test, as they seek to make sense of their experiences and to put some sort of order into their thoughts. The School Curriculum and Assessment Authority (SCAA) takes note of this fact and has given play the prominence it deserves in the Desirable Outcomes for Children's Learning. The document emphasises the need for practical and enjoyable activities and *Junk materials* provides relevant activities across all six identified areas of learning. The ideas are designed to encourage children to extend their skills and knowledge as they explore a multitude of recyclable materials, to recreate new and interesting models and toys which in turn will stimulate and extend their play still further.

Setting up the environment

No specialist knowledge or equipment is needed for the activities in this book and only minimal preparation is necessary. For each activity you will need to provide a clear, comfortable and safe work space for the children, and before beginning you will need to talk to them about the planned activity. In addition you may need to do some preparatory cutting or setting up of equipment, but in every case this is described clearly at the outset and is designed not to be too arduous or time-consuming.

Equipment and storage

Although junk materials are readily available, a good deal of thought needs to be put into their storage in order to avoid them becoming battered and squashed until they are useless. The items which you use on an almost daily basis need to be readily-available and visible (ideally from more than one side) and a wheeled basket that fits below your work surface is a good investment.

If there is space – and finance! – available for more long-term storage, then large, wheeled plastic bins can be obtained in various bright and attractive colours and these are an ideal way of keeping sorted materials safe. Keep one for cardboard tubes, another for plastic bottles or egg cartons, and one for small cardboard boxes, large cardboard boxes or miscellaneous items such as wool and fabric. Smaller stacking boxes or tray units are excellent for less bulky items such as buttons, sweet wrappers or milk bottle tops.

Whether you use sophisticated commercial storage equipment or merely a large cardboard box, clear and descriptive labelling is essential. Use words and pictures, and remember that all sides of your boxes need to be labelled if they can be placed on your shelves in more than one way.

Health and safety

When you receive items, check them carefully before letting the children sort them into their appropriate storage containers. Always check that items are thoroughly clean and free from contamination – if in any doubt throw them out. For hygiene reasons never use toilet roll tubes (use kitchen roll or wrapping paper tubes instead) and only use plastic, not cardboard, egg boxes. Clean plastic containers in a sterilising solution before allowing them to dry thoroughly. Never use any objects with sharp or jagged edges and make sure you obtain, and are familiar with, any Health and Safety Guidelines which may be issued by your local authority as these are usually updated on a regular basis.

Although you will continually remind the children not to put things in their mouths or over their heads, it is still necessary to be extremely vigilant with regard to very small items. Do not use tiny plastic parts that have no ventilation holes however exciting or attractive they may look and NEVER store plastic bags or sheeting within a child's reach. Polystyrene in any shape or form should also be avoided due to the danger of inhalation of tiny particles.

Have regular sorting sessions to ensure that your junk is in good condition and that no unsuitable items have slipped in unnoticed.

Throughout the book, reference to safety issues are highlighted through the use of the word CARE! where potential hazards may be present and where particular care should be taken.

Using adult helpers

Adult helpers are invaluable when young children are working with junk materials. Not only can they help with the practical tasks of organising the work space and ensuring that tools and equipment are used efficiently and with safety, but they can also chat to the children informally as they work, to help them organise their own thoughts and ideas.

Having an interested adult close at hand will encourage even very young children to persevere until the task is complete, while even the most capable child will probably welcome a more dextrous hand when materials are proving a little difficult to handle. A few encouraging words or a piece of practical advice when things are not going to plan will boost the child's confidence and prevent much of the frustration that often leads to failure, thus enabling the child to learn from the experience and be ready to tackle progressively challenging tasks in the future.

Observation and assessment

When the children are playing, it is worth having a notepad close at hand to jot down observations as they occur, rather than relying entirely on your memory. If you can get access to a video-camera, you could record several different groups of children tackling the same task, so that you can observe them later, in a more detached and leisurely manner than is normally possible when you are surrounded by egg boxes, glue and enthusiastically energetic young children! Show the children the recording and help them make their own observations and, later, self-assessments.

Whichever way you choose to observe and assess the children, it is important to remember to focus your attention on only one or two aspects of development at any one time. Consider: safe and efficient use of tools and materials; ability to follow instructions; co-operation with others; willingness to learn; confidence and enthusiasm; perseverance and concentration and the ability to initiate and follow through ideas.

Try to make time for regular recording of your observations and assessments of each individual child so that you get an overall picture of their progress and can choose or adapt future activities to suit their individual needs within the group.

Links with home

Always make the children's carers feel welcome in your group and value their contributions. When dealing with junk materials this is especially important, as they are your regular suppliers and without their help your stocks would soon run dry. Communicate your requirements for junk materials clearly and consider setting up a system of collection that will help you to maintain a varied and interesting supply of usable materials. Perhaps you could put up a notice to say which items you are collecting that particular week or encourage the children to draw pictures or write notes to remind themselves of what to save. Periodically you could send home a list of the types of materials you need and encourage the children to bring them in as soon as they have a bag full.

Make a list of anyone who is able to come in and help in any way and remember to call upon that help regularly so that carers will feel valued. If anyone seems a little uncertain of their ability to help, invite them to call in to watch regular helpers at work and to work alongside them until they gain more confidence.

Also make sure that those parents or carers who are unable to take an active role in the group do not feel isolated. Send home copious messages and notes to keep them fully informed of the group's activities and of their child's progress and remember to invite them to any major events or functions you are planning.

How to use this book

Junk materials contains six activity chapters, each devoted to one particular Area of Learning. Each activity within each chapter is structured in the same way and organised under the same section headings.

First a learning objective is established for each activity within the Area of Learning covered by that particular chapter. Most activities will also overlap into other areas of the curriculum too. For example, language development and social development are constant and on-going processes and are therefore implicit in every activity.

Next a group size is given indicating the number of children who can be actively involved in the set task with one adult supervisor. Use this as a guide which can be adapted to suit your own particular circumstances.

'What you need' lists the materials and equipment required to successfully complete the activity. It too can be adapted to suit your own particular requirements and the availability of materials. Each activity will need some sort of introductory discussion before the children begin work and it will sometimes be necessary to do some advance preparations beyond setting up the work area and collecting the materials. It might also be wise to try any practical tasks yourself, prior to demonstrating to the group, so that you will be aware of any difficulties that might arise and therefore be ready to guide the children to a solution.

The main activity is explained in 'What to do' which provides explicit instructions for the activity, and illustrations are also included for further guidance, where necessary

Suggestions are made of suitable questions to ask the children in order to stimulate them to ask their own questions and to prompt further discussion. Allow time for consideration and discussion of those questions which do arise since such verbalisation often helps to clarify understanding and consolidate any learning which has taken place.

Support for younger or less able children is included as well as ideas for extending the activity for use with older or more able children. It is often a good idea to encourage the children to set themselves challenges that will broaden the scope of the activity and increase their range of skills.

Finally follow-up activities are suggested to broaden and extend the main activity into other areas of learning and to prompt further investigations or activities within the central theme.

One activity from each chapter is accompanied by a photocopiable resource sheet to be found at the back of the book. Some of these are to be used as part of the main activity while others can be used to follow up the work done in that activity. Suggestions for ways in which you can use these sheets are included. For example, you may wish to enlarge some of them to A3 size for use with younger or less able children or you may choose to mount the sheets on card to improve durability.

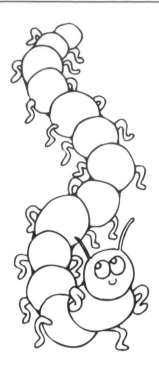

PERSONAL AND SOCIAL DEVELOPMENT

LANGUAGE AND LITERACY

JUNK MATERIALS

KNOWLEDGE AND UNDERSTANDING OF THE WORLD

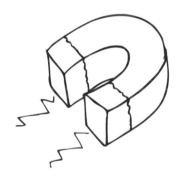

MATHEMATICS

PHYSICAL DEVELOPMENT

CREATIVE DEVELOPMENT

Encourage the children to extend their vocabulary, improve their verbal ability and develop their listening skills as they enjoy making and playing with a variety of interesting objects made from recyclable materials.

PLACE MAT LETTERS

Learning objective
To develop phonic awareness.

Group size
Up to four children.

What you need
A5 paper, A4 paper or thin card, adhesive, old magazines or catalogues, scissors, felt-tipped pens, clear sticky-backed plastic (or access to a laminator).

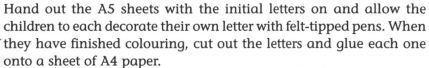

Setting up
Draw the initial letter of each child's name on a sheet of A5 paper. Talk about each letter, naming it and pointing out that it is a capital letter because our names are very important words. Make sure the children can recognise their own initial letters and play games to familiarise them further. Tell them that they are each going to make a place mat using their letters.

What to do
Hand out the A5 sheets with the initial letters on and allow the children to each decorate their own letter with felt-tipped pens. When they have finished colouring, cut out the letters and glue each one onto a sheet of A4 paper.

Next, help the children to search through the catalogues and magazines for pictures of things beginning with their initial sound. Encourage them to look carefully and to keep repeating the sound they are searching for to help them identify suitable objects. Help by tearing out the whole page to make it easier to cut out the picture.

Once several pictures have been glued into position on the place mats finish them off by covering them in clear sticky-backed plastic or laminate them for a really durable finish.

Questions to ask
What is the name of the letter on your mat? What sound does that letter make? Can you think of anything that begins with that sound? Do you think you might find a picture of that thing in this catalogue?

For younger children
They may need a lot of help to cut out their letter.

For older children
Encourage older children to decorate the reverse of their place mat by drawing a pattern made with the capital and lower case versions of their initial letter.

Follow-up activities
● Use the place mats to lay a table for four children – think of things to eat which begin with the children's initial sounds.
● Play reverse I-spy: 'I spy with my little eye… a cat. What does it begin with?'
● Search pages of an old newspaper and see how many times an initial appears.
● Make a collage using single letters cut from old newspaper headlines.

TELEPHONES

Learning objective
To develop talking skills.

Group size
Up to six children.

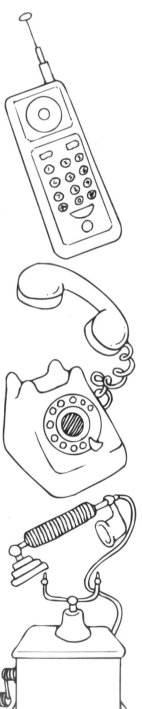

What you need
A collection of different types of telephone both old and new (ask friends and relatives, or try the local recycling centre, the telephone exchange and the local museum's loaning service),small cardboard packets and boxes, coloured sugar paper, pencils, scissors, PVA adhesive, adhesive spreaders, straws, string or wool, small pieces of white paper, felt-tipped pens.

Setting up
Show the children the collection of telephones and ask them to describe the colour, shape, size and materials used. Can they identify the numbers on the buttons? Do they know what the other buttons are for? Ask several children to demonstrate how to use a telephone.

What to do
Explain that the children are going to make their own telephones. Suggest that they base their ideas on one of the real telephones and invite them to each choose a cardboard packet or box to represent their telephone. Use a second box to make a hand set.

Help them to position their chosen box on the sugar paper and to draw round each face of the box/es. Then cut out all the shapes and stick them onto the appropriate face of the box. Use string or wool to represent cords and use straws for aerials. Make buttons for the telephones by writing numbers or symbols on white paper and sticking it onto the covered boxes. The children could also use felt-tipped pens to copy other lines or marks onto their telephone.

Allow the models to dry and then encourage the children to work in pairs, telephoning each other. Encourage them to develop conversations with each other as freely as possible. If necessary, provide some suggestions for simple role-play to help them get started.

Questions to ask
Talk about the shapes produced when drawing round each face of the box. Encourage the children to copy details from their real telephones. Once all the children have had time to use their telephones in pairs, ask for volunteers to demonstrate to the rest of the group.

For younger children
Help the children with the numbers by asking an adult to act as scribe or by providing ready-made numbers for them to use.

For older children
Suggest a detailed role-play situation to each pair (an accident, a fire) and ask them to act out an appropriate telephone conversation.

Follow-up activities
● Make a list of the places where the children have seen a public telephone.
● Use a one minute sand timer to limit the length of the telephone call.
● Use telephone directories in the role-play area.
● Using the photocopiable sheet on page 59, invite the children to use the speech bubbles to write or dictate a conversation.

PLASTIC BOTTLE PUPPETS

Learning objective
To develop story-telling skills.

Group size
Up to six children.

What you need
Small, clean plastic drinks bottles, short lengths of dowelling, Plasticine, PVA adhesive, scraps of paper, card, wool and fabrics, scissors and elastic bands.

Setting up
Demonstrate how a plastic bottle can be inverted onto a piece of dowelling to make the head of a very simple stick puppet. (Remind the children not to insert the dowelling until their puppet is otherwise complete.) Talk about the characters you might make.

What to do
Encourage the children to think about the character they wish to create before they begin, and help them to select their own materials.

Secure the bottles to the table with a lump of Plasticine while they are being worked on to prevent them rolling around. Show the children how to make a hole in the centre of a piece of fabric, put it over the neck of the bottle and secure it with an elastic band to make the puppet's body.

When the puppets are finished, encourage the children to work in pairs to create a simple story to perform for themselves or for an audience of friends.

Questions to ask
Who is your character? What sort of a character is it? Is it a special kind of person – perhaps a queen or a police officer or even an animal? Is it kind or grumpy? Is it lonely or frightened? What might have made it feel that way? What might happen to change things?

For younger children
Use double-sided tape rather than adhesive to avoid the drying time that very young children sometimes find too frustrating to cope with or provide a selection of ready-made features for the children to use.

For older children
Encourage older children to write scripts so that plays can be performed, improved upon and performed again.

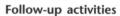

Follow-up activities
● Set up a theatre in the role-play corner with a small stage, numbered seats and tickets for the audience, and perhaps even programme sellers, ushers and ice-cream sellers.
● Make a collection of different puppets – from simple finger-puppets through to complex marionettes.
● Use a selection of clean, plastic bottles for sorting activities.
● Learn to sing 'Ten green bottles'.

BIG BAD WOLF HEADS

Learning objective
To encourage
sequential recall of a
familiar story.

Group size
Up to six children.

What you need
Large cereal boxes, adhesive, grey/brown sugar or wrapping paper, scraps of white and black paper, and grey/brown fur or felt, scissors.

Setting up
Tell the story of 'The Three Little Pigs' (Traditional) and suggest that the children make their own Big Bad Wolf heads.

What to do
Make each child a head by cutting a cereal box diagonally in half across its largest face. Then help the children to cover this basic shape with brown or grey sugar paper – either by drawing around each face of the box, cutting it out and sticking on the four separate pieces, or by covering the box in a thin layer of adhesive and wrapping the sugar paper around it in one piece.

The children can then add ears, teeth, eyes and nostrils before finally embellishing their creature with scraps of fur or felt.

Retell the story, this time allowing the children to wear their heads as they take the part of the wolf. (Pushing the back of the cardboard head inward to make creases down the face, just behind the eyes, and pinching the nose into a point, will give a more realistic appearance and keep the mask in place.)

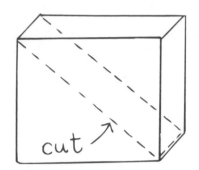

cut

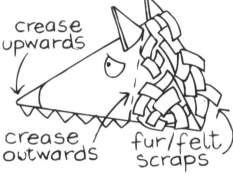

crease upwards

crease outwards

fur/felt scraps

Questions to ask
The wolf was a very fierce creature. How can you make your wolf look fierce? (Encourage the children to experiment with differently shaped eyes and differently positioned ears, before they finally glue them into place.) What do you think his teeth looked like? (Sharp and pointed.) What colour might his teeth be? (White or yellow.)

For younger children
Be aware that some very young children may become distressed by others wearing masks.

For older children
Older children may like to make pig masks and scenery and perform 'The Three Little Pigs' for others to watch.

Follow-up activities
● Use the heads for a retelling of 'Little Red Riding Hood'.
● Investigate different wind-makers such as bellows, balloon pumps and bicycle pumps and try to discover how they work.
● Make a collection of Wolf words (growly, big, cruel, hungry, vicious) and a collection of Little Pig words (terrified, scared, frightened, squealy, brave, trembly).
● Play 'What's the time Mr Wolf?'

HOLIDAY SUITCASES

Learning objective
To encourage the
children to talk about
their own experiences.

Group size
Up to six children.

What you need
Undamaged cereal boxes, PVA adhesive, adhesive spreaders, scissors, holiday brochures.

Setting up
Completely seal up a cereal box for each child and divide the brochures up into separate pages.

What to do
This activity is best done over two or more sessions.

Explain to the children that they are going to make suitcases and talk about what we use these for and the sort of things we might carry in them. Then give each child a sealed box and ask them to cut out and glue brochure pictures onto it to cover it completely. They can then coat all but the base of the box with a thin layer of PVA adhesive and leave it to dry to a strong and glossy finish.

Once the boxes are dry, carefully cut along the centre of two short sides and one long side, creasing along the centre of the second long side to make a hinge and enabling the case to open flat into two halves.

The children can then add two strips of card to make handles, cover the base with its sealing layer of PVA adhesive and leave to dry completely before using the case for various role-play activities.

Questions to ask
While the children are working, encourage them to recap holiday experiences of their own and to compare them with others in the group. (Be sensitive to individual children's circumstances.) Where did they go? How did they get there? Who did they go with? Where did they stay? In a hotel? A caravan? A tent? Or perhaps they lived on a boat?

For younger children
Provide a supply of ready-cut brochure pictures to eliminate the cutting out stage.

For older children
Encourage them to look for suitable words to incorporate into their collage or to cut out individual letters to personalise their case.

covered
with holiday
brochure
pictures

crease
upwards

Follow-up activities
● Learn to fold some clothes to pack into a real suitcase.
● Look at postcards of holiday destinations and draw some things you would need to pack if you went there.
● Make your own postcards to send messages to your friends.
● Pack your suitcase with several small items and use it to play Kim's game.

BOOKMARKS

Learning objective
To encourage the careful handling of books.

Group size
Up to eight children.

What you need
Books (adult as well as children's), old envelopes, scissors, crayons or felt-tipped pens, sticky plastic.

Setting up
Before beginning this activity, spend as much time as possible looking at books and talking about how they are organised. Point out that some books are far too long to read at one time. Ask the children for ideas for remembering which page we are up to when we return to the book later. Discuss the advantages and disadvantages of the various suggestions and finally invite the children to make their own bookmarks.

What to do
Ask each child to choose an envelope and to find on it a corner that has not been spoiled by opening. Help them to draw a diagonal line across that corner and to cut carefully along it. They can then decorate the 'corner' on both sides, thus making a bookmark which can be slipped onto the corner of the page and which will stay in place without spoiling the book.

Be careful not to use felt-tipped pens which smudge, choose bright crayons instead or cover the bookmarks with sticky plastic.

Questions to ask
Why should we not fold the corners of pages? (Because it spoils the book.) Why don't we just leave the book open at the page we are up to? (Because someone else might close it, we can't put it away safely if it is open and it might get spoiled if it is left lying around.) Why should we try to take great care of our books? (So that they will last a long time and can be shared by other people.) Talk about where books come from and how we need to conserve our trees and forests by not wasting paper.

For younger children
Very young children may need help to devise a pattern.

For older children
Older children can be encouraged to make a set of bookmarks for friends or family, personalising them with illustrations reflecting the particular interests of the potential recipient.

Follow-up activities
● Set up a library in the role-play area.
● Design a book cover for your favourite story.
● Visit a library and find out how the books are arranged or how to find a particular book.
● Make a book all about yourself.
● Appoint a 'librarian' to keep the book area tidy.
● Make a list of rules for taking care of books.

INCY WINCY SPIDER

Learning objective
To introduce the idea
of 'opposites'.

Group size
Up to six children.

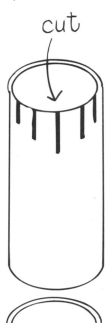
cut

What you need
Cardboard tubes, paint, masking tape, scraps of card, felt-tipped
pens, adhesive, grey, brown or black wool, scissors.

Setting up
Make a model following the instructions below, and use
it to illustrate the rhyme 'Incy Wincy Spider' as you recite
and discuss it with the children. Suggest that they then make
a model of their own.

What to do
Ask each child to select one long tube and one short tube and to
make five cuts around one side of the top edge of the short tube.
Then, using masking tape, attach this edge to the bottom of the long
tube (at an angle of about 60°) to make a drainpipe. Paint the
drainpipe and leave it to dry. Next, ask them to take a piece of
cardboard (roughly A5 size) and fold it in half to draw a large sun on
the front and small raindrops on the back. Sandwich one end of a
piece of wool between the two pictures, gluing them together to secure
it. At the other end, make a spider by folding in half four strands of
wool, wrapping them around the middle and forming a body and
eight legs. When the wet drainpipe is completely dry, thread Incy
Wincy through the tube to dangle at the bottom.

As the rhyme is recited the sun can be slowly raised to let Incy
climb, then turned around for the rain to be quickly lowered to make
Incy fall.

black
wool

Questions to ask
Once the children are familiar with
the rhyme, tell them that things
that are completely different to
each other are called 'opposites'.
Incy climbed up the spout but what
happened when it rained? (He fell
down.) The rain was wet but what did
the sun do to it? (Dried it all up.) Continue to point out pairs of
opposites throughout the activity, asking the children to help you
complete them.

For younger children
They may need help to join the tubes.

For older children
They may like to write out the rhyme and
pin it on a wall alongside their model so
that their friends can play with it as they
read it aloud.

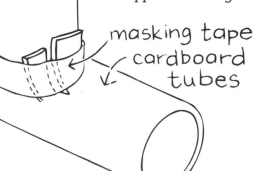
masking tape
cardboard
tubes

Follow-up activities
● Listen to some
music and try to hear
high notes and low
notes.
● Draw a picture of
a street with one half
in daylight and the
other at night.
● Devote a
movement or PE
session to
'opposites'.

PENCIL BOXES

sticky
masking
tape

holes

Learning objective
To foster the understanding that pictures and words carry meaning.

Group size
Up to six children.

What you need
Small, strong, recycled boxes, sticky tape or masking tape, white kitchen paper, adhesive, crayons, an awl or old screwdriver, blunt pencils.

Setting up
Using the awl or screwdriver, pierce holes (about 2cms apart) in the tops of the boxes then seal the tops securely with sticky tape or masking tape to make a solid container.

What to do
Tell the children they are going to make pencil boxes and show them those you have prepared. Encourage them to think for themselves by asking what should be done, rather than giving instructions. Hopefully, someone will soon suggest that the holes need to be made bigger. (This can be done with the blunt pencils.) Look at the outside of the boxes. Discuss the words and pictures on them. What do they tell us? (What was in them.) So what should we put on the outside of our boxes? (The word 'pencils' and pictures of pencils.)

Demonstrate how to cover the boxes by gluing a strip of kitchen paper, lying the box sideways on it and rolling it along, to cover the four sides to make a plain white box. The children can then decorate their boxes appropriately. Discuss whether this needs to be done on one, two, three or all four sides.

Questions to ask
Can you see any other labels around the room. Where are they? What do they tell us? Are they in words or pictures – or a mixture of the two? Taps are labelled to tell us which is hot and which is cold – what are these labels like? (Sometimes in words, sometimes just initial letters and sometimes just coloured dots.) Do the children know what the colours indicate? Can they think of other signs that are just colours? (Traffic lights, wires.)

For younger children
An adult should enlarge the holes to the correct size.

For older children
They may wish to decorate an open-sided box to make an accompanying notepaper-holder.

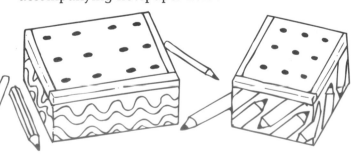

Follow-up activities
● Use a pencil box for number games – take some out and ask your friend how many are missing or take all the pencils out and try to put them in order of size.
● Find out how pencils are made.
● Go for a walk indoors or out and find and read as many signs and labels as you can.

CHAPTER TWO

Help the children to understand more about shapes and their properties as well as counting, measuring and sorting, as they use a variety of materials to produce their own mathematical equipment.

MONEY BOX

Learning objective
To sort and match coins by colour.

Group size
Up to four children.

What you need
Three equal-sized cardboard cylinders for each child, strong adhesive, offcuts of card, felt-tipped pens, silver foil, gold and brown fabric/paint/paper, selection of coins, scissors.

Setting up
Place three cylinders together on a piece of card and draw around the base, leaving a border of about one centimetre, to make a roughly triangular shape which can be used both as a lid and as a template for the base. Cut a 5mm slot from each corner towards the centre for a length of about 2.5cms. Make one for each child.

What to do
Inspect the coins together and talk about what you can see. Notice the differences and similarities between the coins (colour, size, markings, shape). Emphasise that they must not put coins near their mouths and that you will all wash your hands carefully at the end, as coins can be very dirty.

Next, give each child a selection of coins and ask them if they can sort them by colour. Spread out the gold, silver and brown materials in front of the group and ask if they can match the materials to their groups of coins. Hopefully, they will match the £1 coin with the gold paper; the 50p, 20p, 10p and 5p with the silver and the 2p and 1p with the brown.

Next, help each child to cover one cylinder in each of the three materials, make a base, select a lid and glue them together to make a three tube money box. Leave to dry under a book or other heavy object to ensure a good seal between cylinder and lid. Add felt-tipped pen patterns to the lids for a decorative finish.

The completed boxes can be taken home as gifts for the family.

Questions to ask
Which coin is the biggest/smallest? How many corners does the 20p/50p coin have? Whose head is depicted on the coins? One side of the coin is the head but what is the other side called? The queen is wearing a crown – can the children spot a crown on the tail side of the coins?

For younger children
Provide ready-made bases and lids.

For older children
Design boxes to suit their own coin-sorting system.

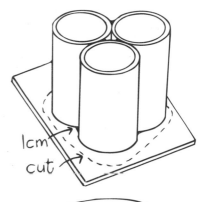

1cm

cut

2.5cm long

5mm wide

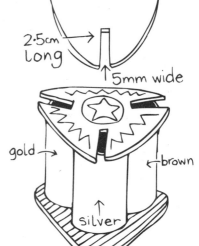

gold

brown

silver

Follow-up activities
● Take Plasticine impressions of the coins.
● Make a pile of the appropriate number of pennies beside each coin.
● Learn to toss a coin.
● Design a coin of your own.

SHAPE HOUSES

Learning objective
To name and describe 2D shapes.

Group size
Up to six children.

What you need
Pictures of houses, small cardboard boxes, paint, paintbrushes, sugar paper, corrugated card, textured wallpaper, felt-tipped pens, strong adhesive, adhesive spreaders, coloured sticky shapes, scissors.

Setting up
Talk together about the pictures of houses. Name and describe the two dimensional shapes on the buildings. Ask the children to identify how many circles/squares they can count on one house.

What to do
Explain that the children are going to make their own houses. Invite them to choose a cardboard box and paint it one colour all over. Allow it to dry before making a roof with sugar paper, corrugated card or wallpaper. Then invite the children to use the sticky shapes to add doors, windows and chimneys. When they have finished, they may like to use felt-tipped pens to add further details such as drainpipes, window-boxes or curtains. Display the finished houses in a row to form a 'street'.

Questions to ask
Refer the children back to the pictures of the houses for ideas. Name and talk about the shapes the children choose to use. What shape will they use for a chimney? Will all the windows be the same shape? How many doors and windows will there be? Describe each shape. How many edges does a triangle have? How many corners does a square have? Compare the lengths of the edges of a rectangle. Remind the children to make all four walls of their house interesting – not just the front. What other features would they like to add and can they think of ways to achieve them? Ask the children to choose which house they like best and explain why.

For younger children
Limit the number of shapes to square, circle, rectangle and triangle only.

For older children
Include more unusual shapes such as hexagons and octagons and suggest that the children cut some shapes in half to make new shapes.

Follow-up activities
● Sort the finished houses – make a set of houses with circles on or a set of houses with square chimneys.
● Go for a walk and look for shapes on local houses and other buildings.
● Draw the outline of a house and use rubber stamp shapes to add features.
● Use the photocopiable sheet on page 60. Invite the children to match the houses with identical shapes.

GIANT DOMINOES

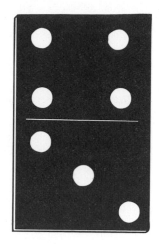

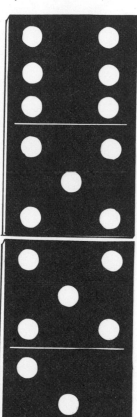

What you need
A set of dominoes, similarly-sized cardboard boxes (tissue boxes are ideal), black sugar paper rectangles to fit the base of the boxes, adhesive, scissors, white paper circles about 2cms in diameter, thin strips of white paper.

Setting up
Look at and discuss the set of ready-made dominoes. Point out that each one has two distinct halves. Count the dots on each half and note how they are laid out in particular patterns. Talk about the dominoes with a blank and discuss the idea of nought/nothing/zero. Allow plenty of time for exploratory play with the dominoes before suggesting that the children make a giant set to share.

What to do
Put aside the seven dominoes which contain a blank for use with very young children or those with counting difficulties. Then ask each child to choose one of the other dominoes to copy. Show them the prepared materials and challenge them to make their own domino.

Talk about their work as it progresses and encourage each child to look carefully at the chosen domino, to count the dots on each separate half and to copy their pattern accurately. (To avoid duplication, ensure that each domino is removed once a giant copy has been made.)

When a complete set has been made, use them for various counting, sorting and matching activities as well as the traditional game.

Questions to ask
Are any of the dominoes identical? (No.) Can anyone find a domino whose two halves are identical? Does anyone know what this sort of domino is called? (A double.) How many dominoes contain a one dot half? (Seven.) How many contain a two dot half? (Seven.) What about three/four/five/six dots? (Seven of each.)

For younger children
Let them choose from the dominoes with one blank half so that they can concentrate on just one amount rather than two.

For older children
Challenge them to sequence all the one-dot dominoes (1:0, 1:1, 1:2, 1:3, 1:4, 1:5, 1:6). Try the same with other amounts.

Follow-up activities
● Use the dominoes for simple sums by adding or subtracting their separate halves.
● Draw a domino using numbers instead of dots 5 3 and see if your friend can find the right one from the set ⋮⋮ ⋰
● Make a set of alphabet dominoes.

JUNK SEARCH

Learning objective
To introduce comparative measurement.

Group size
Up to eight children.

What you need
A good selection of boxes and cylinders.

Setting up
Select two items of different heights and place them on a surface in clear view of all the children. Ask them if they can tell you which item is taller/shorter than the other. Do this several times with different objects before increasing the difficulty level by placing the objects at a distance from one another and lying them on their sides at different angles. Then explain that you are going to play a finding game.

What to do
Select a box or a cylinder, place it on the table and ask the first child to find something that is taller/shorter than this item. Ask the child to demonstrate that he/she is correct (by placing the item next to yours on the table and comparing their heights). Reinforce correct solutions by congratulating the child using appropriate comparative vocabulary.

If a child is wrong, ask if he/she is sure it really is taller and help to measure it against your item. Give this child the opportunity to choose a more suitable object before moving on to the next child.

Repeat the activity, this time comparing widths.

Questions to ask
Many children confuse taller with higher so show them that the objects being compared need to 'share the same base' or 'stand on the same surface'. Can they see anything around them that is taller than themselves? How can they check whether they are right? Stress the negative comparisons (narrower and shorter), which are often more difficult to understand. (Yes you are taller than the cupboard – it really is shorter than you.)

For younger children
They may like to select their own object and set the challenge for the next child themselves.

For older children
Set more complex challenges such as finding an item which is taller but narrower than the first object or shorter but wider than the second.

Follow-up activities
● Ask each child to select ten items and put them in ascending order of height or width.
● Line the children up in ascending size order and record the result in a block graph.
● Make a Plasticine snake as long as the table.

CYLINDRICAL RELIEF

Learning objective
To extend mathematical vocabulary with regard to size and position.

Group size
Up to six children.

What you need
Cardboard cylinders of various sizes (if necessary, cut some to produce a greater variety of lengths), paint, paintbrushes, strong adhesive, brushes or adhesive spreaders, thick paper or thin card.

Setting up
This activity is best carried out in two distinct parts. During the first session, ask the children to paint the cylinders different colours. While they are working talk about the various heights and widths of the cylinders. Leave them to dry thoroughly before beginning the second part of the activity.

What to do
Give each child a piece of card to use as the base and ask them to make an interesting pattern by sticking different-sized cylinders to stand on it. Suggest that they vary their arrangement and don't place two cylinders of the same height or of the same colour next to one another. Encourage them to use as many different sizes as they can.

As they work encourage them to talk about what they are doing and to keep checking that they are fulfilling the height and colour rule. Suggest that each new cylinder is put into position and observed carefully before finally being glued into place. When complete discuss the children's work with them, using some of the questions suggested below.

Questions to ask
Have you used a red cylinder? Where is it? Is it in the middle of your base or near an edge? How many other cylinders are next to the red one? Is the red one taller or shorter than its neighbours? Can you find your widest cylinder? What colour cylinder is beside/behind/in front of it? How many cylinders are narrower than your shortest one? How many are wider than your tallest one?

For younger children
Ensure that the cylinders are of substantially different lengths and widths to make the task easier.

For older children
Restrict the number of colours to four but keep the rule that no two adjacent cylinders should be the same colour.

Follow-up activities
● Using graph paper and four differently coloured crayons, make a patchwork pattern with no two adjacent squares the same colour.
● Play 'Simon says' using positional commands such as 'Simon says put one hand behind/beside/on top of your head/foot/table'.
● Read and enact *We're going on a Bear Hunt* by Michael Rosen (Walker Books).
● Do some paper-weaving to foster the understanding of over and under.

3D SHAPES

Learning objective
To become familiar with some of the properties of cylinders and cuboids.

Group size
Up to 20 children; followed by explorative work in groups of up to four.

What you need
A selection of cuboidal boxes and cylinders, a fairly steep sloping surface (at least 45°).

What to do
Show the children a box and discuss its various properties. Talk about how many faces it has and what shape they are. Count its corners and edges. Do the same with a cylinder. Pile several horizontal cylinders on top of one another and discuss what happens. Try the same with the cuboids and again talk about your observations.

Then introduce the slope. Take a cylinder and ask the children to predict what will happen if you lie it sideways on the sloping surface. Choose a child to test the theory. Then repeat the procedure, this time lying the cylinder lengthways on the slope. Try the same experiments with a box, each time observing carefully and discussing what you have all seen.

Questions to ask
What happens to the cylinder when it is laid on the slope? (It rolls down.) Why might this be? (Because it is round – it has a curved surface.) Does the same thing happen when it is stood upright? (No; it stays where it is or topples over.) Why? (Because its base is flat – not curved.) What does the cuboid do? (It slides.) Why does it not roll? (Because it has flat faces and no curve.) What did you notice when the cylinders were piled up? (They kept rolling apart; there were spaces between them; they fell down if they were touched.) Was this true with the cuboids? (Hopefully not!)

For younger children
Ensure the children fully understand the terms corner, face, edge and curved/flat before you begin the activity.

For older children
Extend the activity by dismantling a box or cylinder carefully to see the 2D shape it was made from.

Follow-up activities
● Use boxes and cylinders for printing and notice the shapes they make.
● Make some tessellations with 2D shapes.
● Use a set of wooden bricks with planks and pieces of stiff card to make slopes and experiment with other geometric shapes such as cones and prisms.
● Construct a robot using only cuboids.

SORTING TRAYS

Learning objective
To learn to sort objects in a variety of ways.

Group size
Up to six children.

What you need
Large and small cardboard boxes, masking tape, scissors, Sellotape, small junk materials such as corks, bottle tops and lids, large buttons, peach stones, sweet wrappers, nuts, bolts and screws.

Setting up
Seal all the boxes and cut each large one through the centre to make two trays. Make a small cut in the middle of one edge of each small box.

What to do
Give the children a prepared tray each and ask them to choose four small boxes to fit inside it. Then show them the cuts in the small boxes and explain that they are the starting places for them to cut each box in half to make little sorting trays.

Once each child has completed a tray, present the mixture of small junk to the group and challenge them to sort it into their trays. Observe the children closely as they work and encourage them to talk about what they are doing.

When they have finished, look at each tray in turn and discuss what you see. Encourage the children to tell the rest of the group why they have put certain items together and why others are in a different section. Or ask the rest of the group why they think things are sorted as they are.

CARE! Warn the children about the dangers of putting small objects in their mouths.

Questions to ask
As the children work chat to them continually and question them informally about their thought processes to find out why they are putting certain items together. Sometimes, what may seem a random or illogical grouping can often prove to be based on sound reasoning. Ask: I wonder why you're putting the milk bottle top with the button? If no answer is forthcoming, make some guesses yourself: is it because they are both round? Or is it that they both have holes in? Or perhaps it's because they are both silver?

For younger children
Provide a criteria for sorting such as by shape or colour.

For older children
Encourage them to use two or more criteria when sorting.

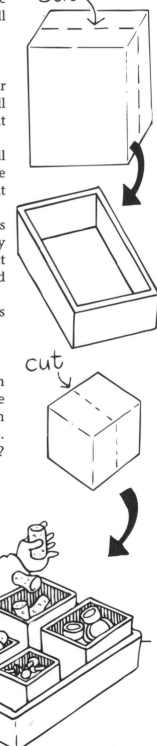

cut

cut

Follow-up activities
● Mix lentils, dried peas, macaroni and rice (CARE!) and challenge the children to separate them using funnels, sieves and colanders.
● Sort some everyday objects by their initial sound.
● Challenge the children to sort a selection of shapes by touch alone.

THE COLOUR TRAIN

Learning objective
To understand ordinal numbers and positional vocabulary.

Group size
Up to 20 children.

What you need
A junk train – paint a selection of boxes different colours and decorate one as an engine.

Setting up
Line the boxes up and place the train in view of the children. Spend time discussing its colours, how many carriages it has and so on.

What to do
Explain that the engine is at the front of the train and that the carriages are all in a line behind it. Tell the children that the carriage closest to the engine is called the first carriage and ask if anyone knows what the next one is called. Continue in this way until all the carriages have been assigned their appropriate ordinal numbers.

Ask questions (see below) of the children and set them a variety of challenges according to their level of understanding, such as 'Move the yellow carriage so that it is second in line', 'put the red carriage behind the green carriage', 'put the blue carriage between the red and the yellow carriages'.

Questions to ask
What colour is the fourth carriage? Which carriage is in front of the third carriage? In which position is the green carriage? Which carriage comes before the second carriage? How many carriages come before the third carriage? Where in the line is the blue carriage?

For younger children
Use only three carriages. It may also be necessary to remove the engine from view to avoid confusion.

For older children
Make ordinal labels to stand in front of each carriage.

Follow-up activities
● Read some of the *Thomas the Tank Engine* stories by Rev. W. Awdry (Heinemann).
● Make a huge junk train, put chairs inside and use it for role-play activities.
● Find out about very old trains and very new ones.
● Use instruments such as scrapers and whistles to make some train music.

CHAPTER THREE

Foster a feeling of self-esteem and tolerance towards others by providing plenty of opportunities to work together as a group for a common purpose in a variety of situations.

TOWERS

Learning objective
To work co-operatively to solve a simple practical problem.

Group size
Up to six children.

What you need
Cardboard boxes of all shapes and sizes.

Setting up
Seal the boxes to make them stronger.

What to do
Challenge the children to work together to build one big tower using every single box you give them. Then give them an assortment of fifteen or more boxes and observe them at work. Encourage them to talk to one another about what they are doing and occasionally make verbal observations yourself but try not to interfere too much with the group dynamics.

When they have completed the challenge (or given up on it!), draw the group together to talk about what they have been doing and what they have or have not achieved. Encourage them to think about the part that they played in the activity as well as what the rest of the group did. Help them to be positive about one another and to recall good ideas or helpful things that were done. Encourage them to think about any problems that occurred and to think of how they could have solved them.

Questions to ask
Have you managed to use all the boxes? If not, then why do you think this was? Was it because you got fed up with it because it kept falling down? (If it was, then encourage them to carry on by offering to help them.) Did you all have a turn to build part of the tower? (If not, do you think that was fair? How could you make sure everybody took part next time you build something together?)

For younger children
Let them work in smaller groups or pairs to begin with.

For older children
Include boxes or shapes that are more difficult to incorporate into a tower such as cylinders or cones.

Follow-up activities
● Challenge the children to build a bridge tall and wide enough for them to crawl under.
● Tell the traditional tale of 'Rapunzel'.
● Sing 'There was a Princess Long Ago' (*Okki Tokki Unga*, A & C Black and in *This Little Puffin* by Elizabeth Matterson, Puffin).
● Paint a town full of very tall blocks of flats and offices.

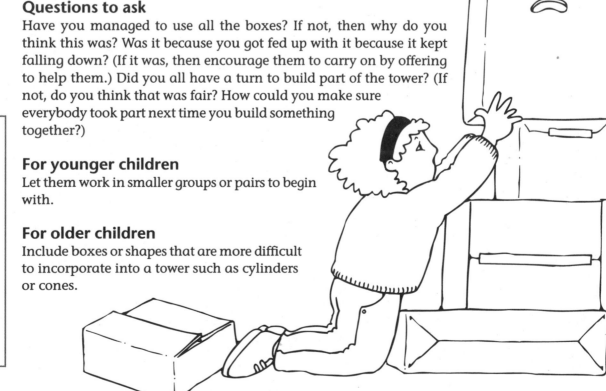

THE BALLOON MACHINE

Learning objective
To learn to work as part of a group.

Group size
Up to six children.

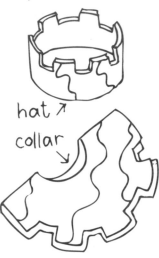

hat ↗
collar ↘

What you need
Three cardboard tubes, large piece of cardboard, two tissue boxes, two yoghurt pots or plastic cups, one cuboidal cardboard box large enough to fit over a child's body, silver foil, strong adhesive or sticky tape, wool or string, an inflated balloon.

Setting up
Cover the tubes, tissue boxes and yoghurt pots in foil. Cut a collar and a hat from card, to represent cogs and cover both in foil. Remove the top and bottom of the cuboidal box, thread string shoulder straps through one end and cover that too in foil.

What to do
Talk to the children about machines and how they have different parts that do different jobs. Explain that if one part of the machine malfunctions then the whole machine fails. Show them the prepared items and suggest that they can be used to make a special machine that can carry balloons without dropping or popping them.

Line up the children and 'dress' each one in a particular item. Pass a balloon to the first child and ask him/her to carefully pass it to the next child, and so on down the line to the end. Encourage each child to think about how they can move and how to pass the balloon successfully to the next child.

wool or string
shoulder straps
↓

Questions to ask
What happens if one child doesn't pass the balloon on successfully? (The machine fails.) What can we do if someone is struggling to pass on the balloon? (Help them by suggesting other ideas for them to try.) Some movements might be much easier to do than others so how can we make sure it's fair for all the children? (Take turns to be different parts of the machine.)

For younger children
Help with suggestions for ways to pass the balloon on and be aware that some young children may be frightened if the balloon should pop.

For older children
Let older children prepare the 'machine parts' themselves and encourage them to think of ideas for additional components.

Follow-up activities
● Develop the activity further by adding repetitive vocal sounds to accompany the robotic movements.
● Use junk materials to print a picture of a machine (try parts of a clock, cotton reels and corrugated card).
● Listen to recordings of every day machines and try to identify the sounds (motor bikes, food mixers, hair-dryers, washing-machines, drills).

CARNIVAL TIME

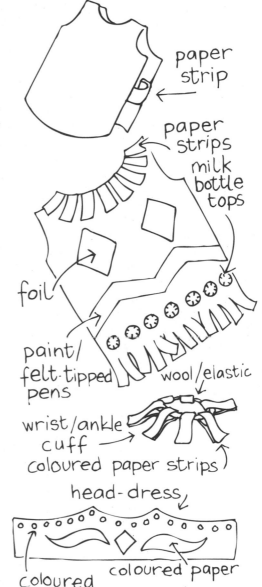

paper strip

paper strips

milk bottle tops

foil

paint/felt-tipped pens

wool/elastic

wrist/ankle cuff

coloured paper strips

head-dress

coloured paper

coloured Cellophane behind Punched holes

Learning objective
To foster a feeling of joy and happiness.

Group size
Up to 20 children for the initial story session. No more than six for the practical activity.

What you need
Nini at carnival by Errol Lloyd (Red Fox), large paper sacks, bright PVA paints or felt-tipped pens, off-cuts of bright paper/card, shiny junk such as clean milk bottle tops, sweet wrappers and foil, wool or shirring elastic, Sellotape, strong adhesive, scissors.

Setting up
Cut head and arm holes in each paper sack and ensure that some of the paper off-cuts are long enough to fit around a child's head.

What to do
Read *Nini at carnival*, which is a story about a young girl who feels sad because she has no costume to wear for the carnival. Her friends come to the rescue and she has a wonderful time. Talk about how happy Nini felt and how good it feels to share our happiness. Suggest that the children make their own costumes and have a happy carnival of their own. Show them the paper sacks and try them on for size. If they prove to be too narrow, slit the sides open and rejoin as tabards.

Encourage the children to think about pattern and symmetry before they begin to decorate their costumes. Help them to position and try out their decorations before finally sticking them into place.

Complete the costumes by making head-dresses or crowns and cuffs for wrists or ankles. Wear the costumes while you dance or play party games.

Questions to ask
Why do people have carnivals? (To celebrate special events.) Can any of the children tell the group about a festival or carnival that they have been to? What did they do/see/hear? How did it make them feel? (Happy, excited, tired, confused.) Can anybody else think of something they have done that made them feel happy? How do you behave when you are happy? (Smile, laugh, hug people, jump up and down, clap hands.)

For younger children
Younger children may find it easier to work on a raised surface such as an easel, rather than a flat work surface.

For older children
Encourage them to plan their designs for their costumes on paper before they begin to make them.

Follow-up activities
● Use old pillowcases to make more permanent costumes.
● Make a set of brightly coloured instruments to accompany the dancing.
● Make a book of 'Things that make me happy'.
● Design posters to advertise your carnival, and make some party food.

ST. GEORGE'S DAY

Learning objective
To find out about an important day in the Christian calendar.

Group size
Up to six children.

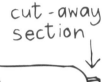

cut-away section

mouth
cardboard tube

egg cartons

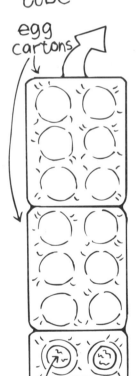

silver foil

cotton wool

What you need
Two cardboard egg cartons and one cardboard tube for each child, strong adhesive, silver foil, cotton wool, red tissue paper, pink, purple, green and black paints, card off-cuts, stapler.

Setting up
Tell the basic story of how there was once a Christian knight who rescued the king's daughter from a fierce dragon and became known as St. George. Talk about how brave St. George was to rescue the young girl and discuss what dragons looked like. Think about their scaly bodies and big eyes, their pointed tails and flaming nostrils.

What to do
Suggest that the children make a really scary dragon to help them remember St. George and his special day on April 23rd. Help them to glue or staple together two egg cartons with their bumpy sides facing upwards and to paint them all over in pink, purple and green. While these are drying, glue the flap of an egg box onto a piece of pink or purple card to make a pair of eyes. Paint the eyes green and leave to dry.

Make a slit in one end of the tube and cut away a section from the other end, leaving a tab. Paint the tube and leave it to dry. Make a card tail and staple it to the end of the body. When all the components are dry, glue the eyes to the front of the body, stuff them with silver foil, attach the nose tube and add red tissue flames and black nostrils with cotton wool smoke.

Questions to ask
Talk about St. George's bravery in rescuing the young girl. Ask the children to imagine what it must feel like to meet such a huge, terrifying creature. What sort of things make you scared? What brave things have you done? (Had an injection, had a filling, slept without a night-light.) How do you feel when you have been brave?

For younger children
Reassure very young children that dragons exist only in stories.

For older children
Older children may wish to invent a humane dragon-trap to avoid unnecessary slaying!

Follow-up activities
● Find out about other Saints such as St. Francis and St. Christopher.
● St. George carried a shield with a red cross on a white background. Design your own shields.
● Read *There's no such thing as a dragon* by Jack Kent (Happy Cat Books).
● Add flames to toy dinosaurs and turn them into dragons to use in the sand tray.
● Paint a dragon on anaglypta paper to give a scaly finish.

FATHER CHRISTMAS POSTBOX

Learning objective
To make a postbox for use at Christmas.

Group size
Up to six children.

What you need
Christmas cards with pictures of Father Christmas, large cardboard box, Stanley knife, large piece of pink card, scissors, red crêpe paper, red and pink sugar paper, stapler, paints, large paintbrushes, cotton wool, PVA adhesive, adhesive spreaders.

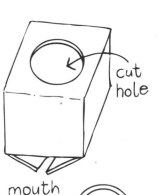

cut hole

Setting up
Show the children the pictures of Father Christmas. Talk about what he looks like and discuss his role during the Christmas celebrations. Also talk about sending and receiving Christmas cards.

What to do
Explain that the children are going to work together to make a postbox shaped like Father Christmas. Place the box with the open-flap side down, for his body. Cut a circle shape in the top of the box with the Stanley knife. (CARE! An adult must do this.) Invite the children to paint the box red.

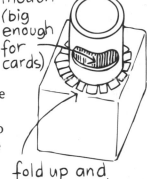

mouth (big enough for cards)

fold up and attach to box

When the box is dry, staple the pink card into a cylinder shape to represent Father Christmas's head and cut a mouth shape (large enough for cards to pass through) with the Stanley knife. (CARE! An adult must do this.) Cut slits around the bottom of the cylinder, fold them up and stick the cylinder to the box. Cut a hat shape from the red crêpe paper and stick it onto the head. Paint on facial features, a belt and buttons. Make arms with two cylinder shapes from the red sugar paper and staple them to the box. Draw round two hands on the pink sugar paper, cut them out and stick them on the end of the arms. Stick cotton wool round his hat, neck and sleeves and add a beard and hair.

red crêpe

cotton wool

When dry, invite the children to post their Christmas cards through the mouth. At the end of each day, take it in turns to lift up Father Christmas, remove the cards, sort and deliver them.

Questions to ask
Refer the children back to the Christmas cards for ideas on what Father Christmas looks like. Where do they think the cards will be posted? (Through his mouth.) Who might they want to send cards to and what should they put on the envelopes? (Friends' names.) Why?(So we know who to deliver them to.)

staple

For younger children
Younger children may need help with the box construction.

For older children
Older children may be able to suggest alternative materials such as curled paper strips for his beard, fabric for his belt or cardboard tubes for his arms.

Follow-up activities
● Design and make cards to send to a friend.
● Use the photocopiable page 61. Invite the children to write names of family, friends or even themselves on the outside of the envelopes and perhaps decorate the envelopes or draw stamps.
● Recycle old Christmas cards by cutting off the pictures, punching holes around the edges and using them for threading activities.

FIREWORK SAFETY FRIEZE

Learning objective
To learn about the dangers of fireworks.

Group size
Up to six children at a time.

What you need
Black or dark blue frieze paper, strong adhesive, cardboard tubes of various sizes, small cardboard boxes of various shapes, chalk, fluorescent PVA paints, glitter, art straws, pinking shears, white paper and felt-tipped pens.

Setting up
Talk to the children about fireworks. Remind them that they are extremely dangerous and should only ever be lit by adults. Talk about sparklers. Remind the children that they should wear gloves, hold sparklers at arm's length and never wave them near people's faces. Invite them to make a frieze to warn everybody to keep themselves safe on Guy Fawkes' night. Using felt-tipped pens on white paper, make a bold caption: 'Please learn: fireworks burn' and put it to one side until needed.

What to do
Ask each child to choose a box or tube to turn into a firework. Then place each one in turn on the frieze paper and draw round it with chalk to mark its position. Using the PVA paints, the children can then decorate their chosen box in bold patterns. While these are drying, position the frieze paper either on a flat surface or across easels so that the children can work on it to add the bright flashes and glittering trails made by their firework. Display the frieze in a prominent position.

When the fireworks are dry, glue them onto the frieze and add art straws to make rocket sticks. Finally, read the ready-made caption with the children and position it below the fireworks.

Questions to ask
Who should light fireworks? (Adults only.) What should you do with spent sparklers? (Drop them into a bucket of water or stick them end-first into a box of sand or soil.) Why should children not play with fireworks? (Because they might get burned.) Also talk more generally about the dangers of fire, playing with matches or lighters.

For younger children
Continue to stress the 'Never play with fire' message throughout the activity.

For older children
Older children could add descriptive words to the frieze – whizz, bang, fizzle, splutter.

Follow-up activities
● Learn how to treat a minor burn.
● Sing the round 'London's Burning' (Traditional).
● Visit a fire station.
● Set up an emergency telephone service for role-play activities.
● Learn your own telephone number and address.

LITTER

Learning objective
To learn to care for the environment.

Group size
Up to six children.

What you need
Disposable plastic gloves, a carrier bag, (litter-pickers are useful but not essential).

Setting up
Talk to the children about litter and the problems it causes. Explain that you are going for a litter-picking walk and discuss the sorts of things you might find. CARE! Remind them that it is dangerous to pick up broken glass or other sharp objects so these must be left for the adult.

What to do
Show the children the gloves and explain that they must not pick up anything without wearing the gloves to protect them from dirt and germs. Then set off on a walk around your building and its surrounding area, collecting rubbish as you go. The adult should carry the bag and supervise which items are put inside it.

Once you have a bag full of litter return to your building, spread out the litter on a washable surface and discuss what you have found. The children should all wash their hands even though they wore gloves. When the activity is complete, dispose of the gloves and the litter and thoroughly disinfect the surfaces you have used. Talk about the dangers of litter and why it is so important to care for the local environment.

Questions to ask
What sort of things have you found? How did the rubbish get there? (It was dropped or thrown down.) What should have happened to it instead? (It should have been binned or recycled.) Have any of the children been to a bottle-bank? Can they explain what it is like? What happens to the bottles deposited there? (They are re-made into new bottles.)

For younger children
Closely monitor what younger children are picking up and take them out in pairs only, to ensure they don't pick up anything they shouldn't.

For older children
Suggest that they sort the rubbish according to the materials it is made of and decide whether or not it is recyclable.

Follow-up activities
● Find out if your local council operates a Green Bank scheme and if it does, consider opening an account.
● Design anti-litter posters to encourage others to keep the locality clean and tidy.
● Sing 'Milk bottle tops and paper bags' from *Someone's Singing Lord* by Beatrice Harrap (A & C Black).
● Set up a collecting box for aluminium cans.

MAKE SOMEONE HAPPY

Learning objective
To think about other people and create a gift for someone special.

Group size
Up to four children.

What you need
A selection of junk materials, fabric off-cuts, a selection of adhesives and sticky tapes, paints and a variety of equipment such as pinking shears, perforators and staplers.

Setting up
Talk about people who are special to us and how important it is to let them know we love them and care for them. Ask the children to think of someone who is very important in their life and to think about a gift they could make to show that person how special they are.

What to do
Invite the children to search through the available materials to help them decide upon a suitable gift. Some children may need help to focus their thoughts so talk about various presents and the people they might be suitable for, and be ready to make a suggestion or two to start them off as they sort through the junk.

Gifts to consider include a pot of flowers or jewellery. A young child might like a toy car to play with or a badge to wear, while a baby might like to watch a mobile twist and turn. Key-rings and bookmarks are always useful and most homes can make room for a decorative box of some sort.

Questions to ask
Who would you like to make a present for? Why? Is it because they have done something special for you and you want to thank them? Or is it just to let them know you care for them? Or is it even to say sorry for something you have done? Is this person an adult or a child? What sort of things do they like? (Useful things, pretty things, things to play with.) What sort of colours do they like? (Bright, dark, light, pastel.)

For younger children
Limit the choices to help younger children to make decisions. Ask: 'Will the present be for Mummy or Daddy?' and 'Would they like flowers or a bookmark?'

For older children
Encourage them to make a greetings card to go with the finished gift.

flowers cut from wallpaper

green washing paper liquid leaves lid

coloured macaroni on shirring elastic

plaited wool

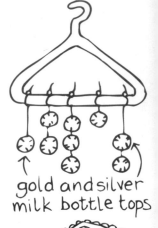
gold and silver milk bottle tops

sequins
drinking straws on sides of lidded box

sunflower seeds on foil covered card

bright card initial
safety pin on reverse

small boxes
foil windows
card discs on drinking straws

treasury tags for keys
small sticky tape centre bound with wool

Follow-up activities
● Use junk to print wrapping paper for the gifts.
● Learn to make twirly bows with florists' ribbon.
● Paint portraits to display in a 'Special People' gallery.
● Think of something you can do to help someone you know.

Encourage young children to take an active interest in the world around them by catching their imagination with water monsters or a giant octopus. Help to develop manipulative skills as they make their own castle or emerging caterpillar from a variety of salvaged materials.

WATER MONSTERS

Learning objective
To explore and select materials to create aquatic monsters.

Group size
Up to four children.

What you need
An old aquarium or a cardboard box model of one, a variety of small junk materials, sand, shells or stones, green crêpe paper, blue Cellophane paper, thread, adhesive, scraps of card and paper, Sellotape, scissors, paint, felt-tipped pens. Pictures of strange underwater creatures would also be useful.

Setting up
Talk about the imaginary world of sea monsters and discuss what they might look like. Study any books or pictures you may have. Show the children the 'tank' and suggest that they make monsters of their own to inhabit it.

What to do
Help the children to think about what they want to make and be ready to suggest ideas if none are forthcoming, but encourage the children to choose their own materials to create their monster. Talk to them throughout the activity, asking plenty of questions to stimulate their imaginations.

Arrange the sand, shells and stones on the bottom of the 'tank' and when the monsters are completed, position them in the tank either on the sandy/stony bed or suspended by thread from the top. Make some plants from green crêpe paper and put them in the tank before finally covering all four sides of the tank with blue Cellophane to give the effect of water.

Questions to ask
What sort of monster are you making? How many legs, if any, will it have? Will it swim around or will it crawl along the bottom of the sea? How many eyes will it have? Will it be friendly or fierce? What colours will it be? Talk about the need for camouflage.

For younger children
They may need considerable help to cut some of the stiffer materials.

For older children
Think up some appropriate names for their creations – the clawed cup-fish, the fringed tube-fish or the one-eyed sock-fish!

egg box section

drinking straws

fringed paper

buttons

cardboard tube

toe of old tights stuffed with newspaper secured with wool and painted.

milk bottle top

old sock stuffed with egg carton strips and painted.

leave top for attaching suspended objects

cut away front, back and sides leaving only frame

shells or stones

pipe cleaner claws

front paper cup cut away for mouth

Follow-up activities
● Make a magnetic fishing game.
● Go pond-dipping and view your specimens through magnifying glasses.
● Make waterproof monsters to go in the water-tray.

THE DARK, DARK HOUSE

Learning objective
To investigate and
explore the properties
of reflective materials.

Group size
Two to three children.

What you need
A small indoor climbing-frame or a huge cardboard box and enough black material to cover it, torches, reflectors, unbreakable mirrors, luminous objects and sparkly items, strong thread, tape recorder.

Setting up
Completely cover the frame or box with black material, leaving one side loose for access. Suspend the various objects from the walls and ceiling of the dark room and place the torches by the entrance. Position the tape recorder close to the house and switch it on as each group enters.

What to do
Explain to the children that you have built them a special house to play in but that it is big enough for only two or three children at a time. Show them the torches and ensure that they know how to work them. Explain that the house is dark but is full of interesting things to see by torchlight. Make sure they understand that they must be very sensible inside as the objects are delicate and might break or fall down. Suggest that they might be brave enough to switch off their torches for a little while inside the house. Be aware that some children may be scared of the dark and need reassurance from an adult.

Now invite the first group of children to enter the house. (Switch on the tape recorder to catch their initial reactions and comments.) After about five minutes, fetch out the first group and let in the next. Chat to the first group about what they saw and felt in the house.

Questions to ask
What was it like in the house? (Spooky, scary, exciting, hot, dark.) What did you see? (Sparkly/shiny things.) Did you switch off your torches? If you did, what did you notice? (Some of the things disappeared but some of them carried on glowing.) Later, when most of the children have experienced the house, play back the tape to see if the children can recognise themselves and whether it sparks off further memories.

For younger children
Very young children may need to be accompanied by an adult at first.

For older children
They may like to compose poems about the dark house.

Follow-up activities
● Make some more things for the house with foil, glitter, Cellophane and so on.
● Talk about reflective clothing with regard to road safety and set up a display of relevant items.
● Go for a walk in search of reflections – in puddles, windows, car doors, etc.
● Make a collection of shiny things – kettles, spoons, buckles and new coins.

FROM CATERPILLAR TO BUTTERFLY

Learning objective
To use skills such as folding and cutting to make a simple model.

Group size
Up to six children.

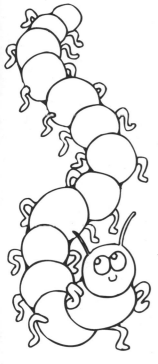

cut away

What you need
Old brown wrapping paper, cardboard egg boxes, paper, scissors, felt-tipped pens, paint or crayons.

Setting up
Cut egg boxes into strips of three segments and make an inverted V-cut in each front segment. Trim them neatly. Talk about the caterpillar and how it becomes a chrysalis which eventually opens to reveal a butterfly or moth and tell the children they are going to make models of caterpillars turning into butterflies.

What to do
Invite the children to each select two egg box strips. Show them how to join them together with an overlap to make a caterpillar, which they can decorate with pens, crayons or paints, adding paper antennae and eyes as desired.

While these are drying, demonstrate to the children how to fold and cut a piece of paper to make a butterfly (20cm wingspan is about right) and encourage them to decorate it as colourfully as possible. Once these are complete, demonstrate how to loosely roll a sheet of brown paper to make a roughly cylindrical shape. Finally, show the children how to roll up the butterfly and secretly place it in one end of the cylinder.

They can then show a friend their caterpillar and tell them how it turns into a chrysalis (child pushes caterpillar in the empty end of the cylinder) and when it is ready it becomes a beautiful butterfly (child pulls butterfly from tube and gently unwraps its wings).

Questions to ask
While the children are making their butterfly, talk about the pattern being symmetrical. Ask them if they can make both top wings the same as each other and both bottom wings identical. Are they sure they have used the same shapes *and* colours *and* positions? How could they be sure opposite wings do match? (They could build up the pattern on each wing motif by motif, checking colour and position as they go.)

For younger children
They may need help to cut out the butterfly without unfolding it and losing the symmetrical shape.

For older children
They may be able to fold the butterfly's wings down to give a V-shaped body section which can be held so that the creature flaps its wings as it is moved up and down.

Follow-up activities
● Provide mirrors and encourage the children to further investigate symmetry.
● Read *The Very Hungry Caterpillar* by Eric Carle (Picture Puffin).
● Use photocopiable activity sheet 62 to learn about the butterfly's life cycle.

FRAMED FAMILIES

Learning objective
*To stimulate discussion
about families.*

Group size
Up to six children.

What you need
Cereal boxes, scissors, single hole perforator, bodkins, thick, coloured wool or raffia, paper, pencils and crayons or felt-tipped pens, adhesives, scraps of braid, ribbon and lace.

Setting up
Cut rectangles of card from the cereal boxes (A5 size) and remove the centres to leave a frame of about 2.5cms. (Use a single hole punch to start the cutting to avoid folding the card.)

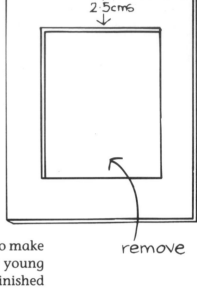

2.5cms

remove

What to do
Talk about families (the people that share the child's house) and invite the children to draw pictures of them. Be sensitive to any individual children's circumstances at home.

Suggest that they use the frames you have made to make an outline to draw within to get the right size (very young children may need help with this). When they have finished their drawings they can glue them to the frames before backing them onto more scrap card from the cereal boxes. Then invite them to decorate their frames with felt-tipped pens, scrap materials such as lace or braid or to perforate the edges and use thick, brightly coloured wool or raffia to bind them.

As they work, encourage the children to ask one another questions about their families to help them understand how they all differ.

braid

felt-tipped pen

Questions to ask
Families can be very complex structures so remember to keep your questions objective and non-judgmental. How many people live in your house? What are their names? How many grown-ups are there? And how many children? Who is the youngest person in your house? Do you have a sister? What is her name? Does she have a sister? Does your Mummy have a daughter? Who is that?

For younger children
Use an A4 size frame for very young children.

For older children
Encourage them to write the name of each person on their drawing.

raffia or wool

Follow-up activities
● Ask the children to write or scribe a few words about their families and display them alongside the finished portraits.
● Make a collection of family portraits, old and new, painted and photographic, to compare and discuss.
● Make a chart to show the various family sizes within the group.

CASTLES

Learning objective
To foster an interest in the past.

Group size
Up to six children.

What you need
Books and pictures about castles, cardboard boxes, tubes, paper cups, washing-up liquid bottles, cardboard egg boxes, scissors, strong adhesive, masking tape and paints.

Setting up
Look at the books and pictures and discuss castles. Point out features such as arrow-slits, turrets and battlements. Find out if any of the children have visited a castle and encourage them to tell the rest of the group about it.

What to do
Invite the children to construct a castle, using a large square box as the base. Explain that castles were usually symmetrical, so encourage them to find and position the various parts before they begin to glue them into place.

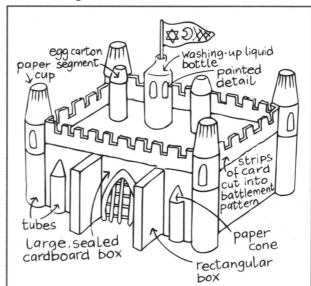

Talk to them about what it must have been like to have lived long ago when there was no running water, no glass in the windows and no electricity. Encourage them to ask questions to find out more and suggest that they might like to study the books and the pictures later, while they are waiting for their models to dry.

Once the glue is dry the children can paint the models.

Questions to ask
What was it like inside a castle? (Dark, cold and damp.) What did the people use to light their way? (Candles and flaming torches.) How did they cook their food? (Over the fire.) How did they make fires? (With small, dry sticks and then twigs and logs.) If the children come up with questions that you cannot answer fully, ask them how they think you could find out more? (From information books.)

For younger children
Secure glued components with masking tape until they are dry to keep parts in places and to avoid the constant dislodging that can occur when young children are working.

For older children
Provide wooden spills or strips of card for the children to make a portcullis and thin string for them to construct a drawbridge.

Follow-up activities
● Populate your castle with play people and animals for role-play activities.
● Design and paint a flag for the castle.
● Furnish your home corner as a castle – with an open fire, roasting spit, metal and wooden bowls and cutlery, sheepskin rugs and twig brooms.
● Visit a castle.

MATCH A COLOUR

Learning objective
To match and name
colours correctly.

Group size
Up to four children.

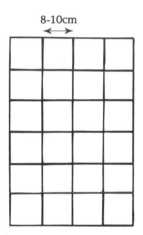

← 8-10cm →

What you need
Scraps of paper or card in eight colours,
24 clean yoghurt pots.

Setting up
Cut out three circles from each colour
card and glue one circle inside each pot.

What to do
Talk about the different colours inside
the pots. Explain that you are going to
play a game where the children must

find two pots with matching colours. Make sure all the children
understand what is meant by 'matching' and let everyone have a
turn to find some pairs.

Then invert the pots, jumble them up and re-arrange them into six
lines of four. Invite the first child to select two pots where the colours
match. Check if the child is correct and ask what the colour is. If the
child has correctly matched the two colours and can name the colour,
he/she keeps the pots and has another turn. If the child is incorrect,
replace the pots in their original position and play passes to the next
player.

Carry on until eight pairs have been won, leaving eight pots
inverted on the table. The child who collects the most pots is the winner.

Throughout play, encourage the children to lift each selected pot
and say the relevant colour aloud, before replacing it as accurately
as possible to help everyone remember where it is.

You may find it useful to make a base grid for children who have
difficulty concentrating.

Questions to ask
Help the children to take their turn slowly and carefully and ask
memory-jogging questions to help them along. Do you remember,
Mark picked up a blue pot just now – can you remember where it
was? Was it in the top row? Or was it perhaps in a corner? What
colour have you picked up? (Yellow.) What colour do you need to
match it? (Yellow.) Who picked up a yellow pot before? And where
did she get it from?

For younger children
Limit the activity to only six different colours, giving the children
more chances to get the 12 matching pairs.

For older children
Make matching pairs of pots, using light, medium and dark shades
or more unusual colours such as grey, beige or burgundy.

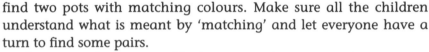

Follow-up activities
● Play the game
using shapes or
numbers instead of
colours.
● Learn the colours
of the rainbow in
sequence.
● Play colour I-spy.
● Choose a colour
and see how many
objects you can find
to match it.
● Make different
patterns using bricks
of only two colours.

ATTRACTIVE JUNK

Learning objective
To explore magnetism.

Group size
Up to six children.

What you need
Various magnets, strong adhesive tape, thick card, scissors, two cardboard boxes containing tin foil, tin lids, keys, empty cans, pieces from old clocks or watches and a selection of non-magnetic junk.

Setting up
Seal the cans with tape or a thick cardboard lid to avoid sharp edges. Arrange the junk on a table with the magnets nearby.

What to do
Allow the children plenty of time to investigate the junk in conjunction with the magnets, observing them as they work. Give them at least 15 minutes to find out how the magnets work. Then draw the group together for a short discussion.

Explain that objects which are attracted to the magnet are called magnetic and those which are not, are called non-magnetic. Then ask each child to select a piece of junk and invite them to say whether they think it is magnetic or non-magnetic. Let them test with a magnet to see if they were correct.

Reinforce correct answers by repeating and extending the child's statement – 'Well done! Yes, your can did stick to the magnet, so it is magnetic.' If a child guesses wrongly, let him try again by taking another guess or selecting another piece of junk and trying again.

Once all the children have had two or three turns, suggest that they might tidy away by using the magnets to sort the junk into two boxes – magnetic and non-magnetic items.

Questions to ask
What happened to some of the junk when you put the magnet near it? (It stuck to the magnet.) Why did it stick? (Because it is magnetic.) What happens if you slowly move a strong magnet towards some magnetic junk? (It makes the junk move.) What happens if you slowly move one magnet towards another magnet? (It jumps, twists or turns it.)

For younger children
Work alongside very young children throughout the activity to help them formulate their thoughts.

For older children
Introduce words such as attracts, repels, poles and iron.

Follow-up activities
● Make a magnetic fishing game from scraps of card, paper or fabric and paper-clips.
● Test the strength of magnets: see how many strung-together paper-clips they can lift.
● Bury objects in sand and try to find them with magnets.
● Make a collection of things that use magnetism – toy trains, construction sets, key-holders, torches, memo-holders, soap-holders, door catches.

A GIANT OCTOPUS

Learning objective
To foster an interest in the world beneath the sea.

Group size
Up to eight children.

What you need
Old, clean nylon stockings or tights, newspaper, cardboard cylinders, strong adhesive, paint, books and pictures of an octopus, bodkin, strong thread, scraps of paper, black felt-tipped pen, blue fabric.

Setting up
Slice the cylinders into 1cm rings and cut the legs off three pairs of tights, retaining one pair intact.

What to do
Tell the children you are going to make a huge octopus by scrunching up newspaper and stuffing it into the legs of old tights. Look at a picture of an octopus and count its tentacles. Notice how flexible the tentacles are and advise the children not to stuff the tights too full or they might become rigid.

Show the children how to separate and open the pages of the newspapers, scrunch them and stuff them down into the toe of the tights. Give six children the task of each filling a single leg. Give the remaining two children the intact pair of tights to share. Once all the legs are filled but still flexible, help the children to stuff the body of the intact pair of tights to make the octopus's head.

Assemble the octopus using the bodkin and strong thread before inviting the children to glue the card rings onto the underside of the tentacles to represent suckers.

When the glue has dried paint the octopus all over in shades of green and grey. Add paper eyes and perhaps a cheeky grin and display the creature by arranging it with splayed tentacles on a piece of blue fabric to represent the sea.

Questions to ask
While the children are working encourage them to talk about the octopus. What might it like to eat? How might it move? Is it friendly or fierce? Where does it sleep? How might we find the answers to these questions? (From information books.) Encourage the children to ask questions of their own and jot them down to refer to later.

For younger children
Young children may need help to push the newspaper into the tights without crumpling it too tightly.

For older children
Older children will be able to sew together the octopus themselves with very little help (but under close supervision!).

Follow-up activities
● Suspend fishes from the ceiling, surround the octopus with seaweed, starfish and crabs to create an undersea world.
● Use wax-resist techniques to make undersea pictures.
● Make some fish cakes to eat.

tights
oversew waist ↓ closed
secure with strong thread
newspaper stuffing
cardboard rings
single legs of tights ↗

CHAPTER FIVE

Promote positive attitudes towards a healthy and active life by turning your junk into toys that develop physical skills such as throwing and catching, jumping and balancing. Develop the children's manipulative skills with threading and joining activities.

CONE AND BALL

Learning objective
To help develop hand-eye co-ordination.

Group size
Up to six children.

What you need
Cones (cut out circles – approximately 15–20 cms diameter – of strong card from cereal boxes or similar), stapler, wool or thin string, newspaper or small airflow balls, adhesive tape, adhesive plastic, felt-tipped pens.

Setting up
Make cones from quadrants of strong but pliable card and balls from tightly-scrunched newspaper.

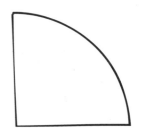

What to do
Tell the children you are going to make a throwing and catching toy using a cone, a ball and some wool. Demonstrate by cutting a piece of wool (measured from nose to finger-tips) and taping it inside the top lip of the cone and tying or taping the ball to its other end. Then flick up the ball and try to catch it in the cone. Help the children to measure their own wool and construct their own toy.

Once the toys are ready the fun can begin. Be ready to suggest ideas to further develop the activity as the children become more proficient or to help those who find it difficult. For a more permanent finish decorate the cones and cover them in transparent adhesive plastic.

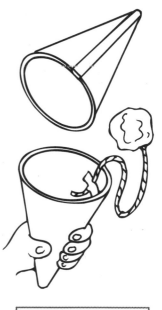

Questions to ask
Can you catch the ball every time you try? Can you do it using the other hand? Can you do it using both hands together? Can you do it with a completely straight arm? Or with your arm raised out to the side? What about with closed eyes? What happens if you use a much longer piece of wool? (This makes the task more difficult.)

For younger children
Generally-speaking, the shorter the wool the easier the task so make adjustments accordingly.

For older children
Encourage them to set their own challenges – perhaps setting time limits or racing to make ten catches.

Follow-up activities
● Use cones and balls to invent a variety of games – stand inverted cones in sand and try to throw small balls into them or balance large balls on small cones for an egg-and-spoon type race.
● Use the cones with a variety of other boxes and cartons for a large scale construction set.
● Investigate the properties of cones by using them as loud-hailers, ear-trumpets (no shouting!) or funnels.

ROBOTICS

What you need
Cereal boxes, aluminium foil, strong adhesive, adhesive tape, buttons, cogs, small wheels, cardboard egg cartons, paper and card off-cuts, card tubes, sequin waste, string, scissors, a selection of simple percussion instruments such as chime bars, scrapers and shakers.

foil taped or glued on

Setting up
Cut out two-thirds of one side of each cereal box, leaving the open flaps attached at the bottom if possible. Cover each box in foil. Talk about what robots are and how they move.

What to do
To make the heads: show the children how to pull the boxes onto their heads using the base flaps so that their faces appear at the open side. Invite them to create their own robot heads using the prepared boxes and a selection of the small junk materials you have available. As the children work, encourage them to talk about what they are doing and be ready to make card cogs and paper springs to supplement any depleting stocks as you go along.

To use the heads: call the group together in a large space and again talk about robots. Introduce the children to the instruments and decide upon a different movement for each one – a chime bar might signify a turn of the head while a scraping sound might accompany the sliding of a foot. Once the children are familiar with the sounds and movements, invent a dance by playing the instruments in a repetitive sequence. Explain that the instruments are the buttons that make the robots move, so the children must be careful to move only when a sound is made and to stop as soon as the sound stops.

lower 2/3 removed

flaps for pulling on head

Questions to ask
Where do robots get their energy? (From batteries or power-packs.) What might happen if these begin to wear down? (The robots may slow down or perhaps malfunction. Practise this.) How do robots move? (Stiffly and precisely.) Often robots have wheels on the soles of their feet, so how might they move along? (By keeping their feet on the floor and sliding them along.)

button

paper spring
sequin waste
paper cog

stri[ng]

egg box sectio[n]
card tube

For younger children
Try using double-sided tape in place of adhesive to eliminate drying-time for impatient youngsters.

card off-cut

For older children
Encourage them to work in pairs to invent their own sequential robot dance.

TUNNELS

Learning objective
*To move with
confidence and
imagination in a
controlled way.*

Group size
Up to four children.

entrance/
exit

What you need
Large cardboard boxes (at least 60cms square), strong adhesive tape.

Setting up
Open or remove the ends of the boxes to make square tunnels and tape them together to form a network.

What to do
Invite the children to explore the tunnel system but warn them that the boxes may not withstand rough treatment so they must try to move slowly and carefully through them so that they don't tear or collapse. Remove shoes before the children start.

After several minutes, gather the group together to talk about what they have been doing, and invite suggestions for moving in different ways through the tunnels. Then allow time for further exploration before again drawing the group together to discuss their discoveries or to watch one another's different ways of moving.

Questions to ask
What was it like in the tunnels? (Dark, cramped, warm, scary, spooky.) How did you go through them? (They probably crawled during their first explorations.) What did you do if you met someone coming the other way? (Had to back up or squeeze to one side to get by.) How else might you go through the tunnel? (On tummies or backs, pushing or pulling with either arms, legs or both.) Do you think you could go backwards through one of the tunnels? And could you go backwards into one end of a tunnel and come out forwards at the other end?

adhesive
tape
entrance/
exit

For younger children
Be aware that some very young children may become frightened in a long, dark, tunnel so leave spaces at the end of each section for them to pop up and look around or cut little windows to let in more light.

For older children
Encourage them to make their own tunnel network – perhaps joining boxes to make longer tunnels or using narrower boxes for added difficulty.

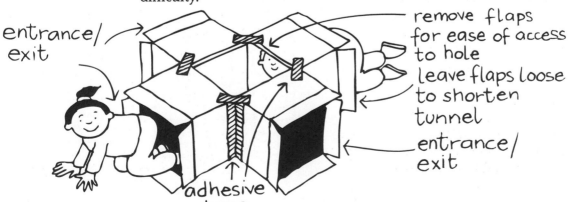

entrance/
exit

remove flaps
for ease of access
to hole
leave flaps loose
to shorten
tunnel
entrance/
exit

adhesive
tape

Follow-up activities
● Use paint-rollers and bright paint to decorate the outside of the tunnels.
● Find out about animals that live in tunnels.
● Build a network of tunnels in wet sand.
● Make your own tunnels for toy trains, boats or cars to go through.

SKITTLES

Learning objective
To practise rolling a
ball accurately and
with control.

Group size
Up to six children at a
time.

What you need
Six plastic drinks bottles with tops (1 or 2 litre size), strong adhesive, strips of fabric about 2cms wide, sand, funnel, 12cm diameter ball.

Setting up
Invite six children to each make a skittle by gluing fabric strips around a bottle in a circular or spiral pattern. Coat with a layer of white adhesive to act as a varnish. Leave to dry until it becomes transparent.

What to do
Show the whole group the decorated bottles and the ball and ask for suggestions of what they might be for. When the correct solution has been given, stand the skittles in a triangular formation and ask for a volunteer to show you how to play the game. Then invite groups of six to take turns to roll the ball at the skittles to see how many they can each knock down. Encourage them to watch carefully to see where the skittles are hit and which way they fall.

Gather the whole group together again to talk about what they have been doing and discuss any observations they have made.

Funnel a few centimetres of sand into each bottle and secure its lid, then stand the skittles up again for a second round of the game. Again gather together and discuss what differences, if any, they have noticed in the skittles now they have been weighted.

Questions to ask
What happens when a ball hits an unweighted skittle? (It knocks it over.) Is this always the case? (Probably – though not necessarily!) Is the same thing true once the skittles have been weighted? (Probably not.) Why is this? (Because the sand makes the skittle heavier.) So how must you roll the ball to knock it down now? (Harder.)

For younger children
Use a bigger ball and make sure the space between the skittles is less than its width.

For older children
Encourage them to write out a list of simple rules to make the game run more smoothly.

triangular
skittle
formation

Follow-up activities
● Stick numbers on the skittles and use them to add up scores.
● Use photocopiable sheet 63 for some careful counting and colouring practice.
● Test different skittle formations and try gently bouncing the ball at them or use a bean bag instead.
● Play table skittles.

I CAN DO IT!

Learning objective
To practise manipulating a wide variety of fastenings.

Group size
Initially the whole group.

What you need
A selection of old, clean clothing with a wide variety of fastenings – zips, toggles, buttons with horizontal/vertical buttonholes or loops, plastic/metal press studs (all sizes), Velcro, laces, shoe buckles, belt buckles, dungaree suspenders, hooks and eyes, press studs.

Setting up
Arrange the clothes on a large table and gather the group around.

What to do
Invite a child to select a garment from the table and show it to the whole group. Talk about what it is and how it is worn. Then look at its fastening and talk about how it works.

Find a volunteer to try on and do up the garment unaided. Encourage the child's efforts and provide verbal assistance if necessary. If the volunteer succeeds offer praise, if not ask for a second volunteer to help. If this child fails too, demonstrate the procedure to the whole group and suggest that they might all like to practise it later.

Go through the whole process again with a different garment and a different fastening. Repeat this a few times before finally telling the children that you are going to leave the clothes there for them to come along and practise fastening whenever they like.

Questions to ask
What is this sort of fastening called? How does it work? Have you got a similar fastening on any of your own clothes? Can you do it up by yourself? Can you undo it? Can you work the fastening when someone else is wearing the garment? (This is often easier since they can look straight at the fastening rather than down on it from above.) If you can, what do you think you might do next time you are stuck with a fastening? (Ask a friend to help.) What if your friend is stuck? (Offer to help.)

For younger children
Start with a small selection of clothes and build up the range as more skills are acquired.

For older children
Encourage them to tackle a new skill daily until they can do them all.

Follow-up activities
● Make a group book 'I can do up/undo...' and let the children contribute a picture of a fastening which they can manage.
● Make collage people, putting a real zip, buckle or buttons on their clothes.
● Play 'Musical Clothes' by passing round a bag of clothes and when the music stops putting on and doing up one of the garments.
● Investigate ways of fastening card or paper together – paper-clips, treasury tags, split rings, paper fasteners.

STILTS

Learning objective
To practise balancing
skills.

Group size
Up to six children.

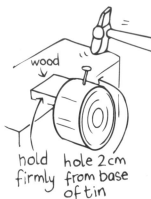

hold hole 2cm
firmly from base
of tin

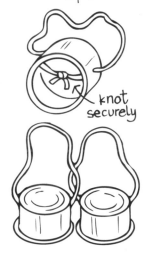

knot
securely

What you need
Six pairs of sturdy 15cm high tins with lids (such as coffee tins),
hammer and nail, an offcut of wood, a table-top and a strong friend
(or a workbench with vice!), lengths of thin rope or thick string just
over a metre long (about the height of the child).

Setting up
Pierce holes in opposite sides of each tin (about 2cms from the
base), by inserting one end of the wood in the tin and getting
another adult to hold the other end firmly down on the table
while you hammer the nail through the tin. Make up five pairs of
stilts by threading a length of string through the holes and knotting
them securely inside the tins. Put the remaining pierced tins and rope
to one side for later use. Hammer the lids firmly back into place and
the stilts are ready.

What to do
Show the children the stilts and talk about what they might be and
how to use them. Then ask for suggestions as to how they were made,
before demonstrating this using the pair of pierced tins that you put
aside earlier.

Invite the children to try out the stilts in a large open
space while you observe and be ready to offer
encouragement, praise or advice as necessary.

Questions to ask
What do stilts make you do? (Make you taller.)
How does it feel when you first stand on the
stilts? (Scary, wobbly, not very safe.) Can you
move quickly on them? Can you walk
backwards or sideways? Is it easier to take
big steps or small steps? Can you stand up
straight and look where you are going as you
walk, instead of bending forwards and
looking at your feet? Can you walk along a
straight line? And along a very wiggly one?

For younger children
They may need several short practice
sessions before acquiring this skill.

For older children
Suggest they devise an obstacle
course using cardboard boxes to
step over, squeeze between or walk
round without stopping or stepping off
their stilts.

Follow-up activities
● Watch a real stilt-
walker at work.
● Use wooden
blocks and planks to
make other things to
balance on like
stepping-stones or
beams.
● Balance on one
leg for a whole
minute.
● Paint a giant
circus picture with
tight-rope walkers,
trapeze artists,
balancing acrobats
and stilt-walkers.

HURDLES

Learning objective
To practise jumping.

Group size
Up to 15 children.

What you need
Long cardboard tubes, pairs of sturdy cardboard boxes of various sizes, adhesive tape, pointed scissors, acrylic paints, a large open space (indoors or out), self-adhesive labels, felt-tipped pen, children with bare feet or pumps.

Setting up
Seal all the boxes with tape and decide which is to be the top of each identically-sized pair. Using the pointed scissors, cut into the centre of a top edge of each box and use this as a starting-place to cut out a curved section approximately 4cms across and 1cm deep. Paint the hurdles with acrylic paints for a more durable finish.

What to do
Rest each end of a cardboard tube in the grooves across the top of a pair of boxes to make a hurdle and invite the children to take turns to jump over it. CARE! Make sure an adult is with the children at all times. Then suggest that they might like to set up a whole course of hurdles of varying heights, using the prepared boxes and tubes.

Once the course is complete, decide in which order the children will work around it and stick numbered labels onto the boxes in the appropriate order. Again invite the children to take turns to tackle the course. After several minutes gather the group together and talk about what they have been doing.

Then rebuild the course in a different order, re-numbering where necessary. Again let every child complete the course before coming together for a final discussion.

Questions to ask
What happens if you are too close to the hurdle when you try to jump it? (You kick the tube off the boxes.) Why should you not get too close to the person in front of you? (Because you may get kicked or crash into them.) Did you manage to jump every hurdle cleanly? Can you jump the hurdles leading with your left foot? And your right? Can you jump over them with both feet together? Forwards? Backwards? Sideways?

For younger children
At first use the boxes lying flat so as to make hurdles only 6cms or so high.

For older children
Try spacing the hurdles evenly and encourage the children to adopt a real hurdling pattern – 1 2 3 hurdle, 1 2 3 hurdle.

cut out section from here

seal box for strength

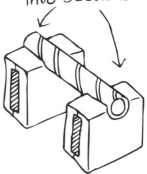
place tube into sections

Follow-up activities
● Let the children feel their heartbeats before the exercise and again afterwards and notice the difference.
● Watch a gymkhana or a real hurdling event – either live or on video.
● Try to find other ways of getting over the hurdles – stepping backwards, high forward-rolling, cart wheeling (with appropriately cushioned landing areas!).

TREASURE CHEST

belt →
milk
bottle
tops →
card →

Learning objective
To use a range of
materials safely and
with control.

Group size
Up to six children.

What you need
Large macaroni or threadable pasta, buttons, shirring elastic, foil,
milk-bottle tops, foil yoghurt pot lids, wool, card discs, ball-point pens,
black shoe polish, paper tissues, bodkin, sequins, sweet wrappers,
glitter, adhesive, small safety pins, strips of stiff paper, cardboard tubes,
fluorescent paints, awl, adhesive tape, scissors.

Setting up
Discuss what constitutes treasure and where it might be found.

What to do
Tell the children you are going to make some treasure of your own.
First establish some safety procedures for using equipment such as
the awl and the bodkin CARE! Ensure that the children are supervised
throughout whilst using small objects. Try some of these ideas:
Medallion: use a ball-point pen to etch a pattern onto the printed
side of a foil yoghurt pot lid. Place a smaller cardboard disc on the
pattern and wrap the edges over to secure it. Wipe a tiny amount of
black shoe polish on the pattern on the silver side of the lid then rub
it off gently with a tissue to give a pewter-like finish. Thread with
wool to make a medallion or attach a safety pin to make a badge.
Armlet: cut spiral strips from cardboard tubes and paint them brightly.
Necklaces and bracelets: thread painted macaroni, buttons or
milk-bottle tops onto shirring elastic (for bracelets) or wool (for
necklaces). Make these sufficiently long to fit around the children's
necks safely and warn them to take care when wearing them.
Belts and crowns: cut strips of card to fit the children's heads and
decorate with sequins, sweet wrappers and milk bottle tops.
Coins: cover card discs with foil or gold sweet wrappers.

While the children are working talk about the way they are
handling the tools and materials and continually remind them of
the safety rules. Once the treasure is made, set up a lovely display.

Questions to ask
Why must you be careful to watch the bodkin all the time you are
using it? (So you don't stab someone.) Why should you not run around
with scissors in your hand? (In case you fall and injure yourself or
others.) What should you do after using paint or glue? (Wash your
hands.) Why? (In case you later put your fingers near your mouth.)

For younger children
Help a very young child to use a bodkin by ensuring that a supervising
adult sits close by and that the child sits with his back to a wall.

For older children
Draw up a simple illustrated list of safety rules to display near the
work area, for the children to refer to.

medallion
foil
lid
folded
over
card
disc

raised
pattern

paint or
decorate brightly

armlet

necklace
wool →
pasta →

bracelet
buttons →
shirring
elastic →

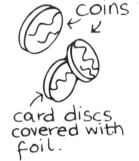

belt
foil
cellophane
sweet
wrappers

milk
bottle top

coins →
card discs
covered with
foil.

Follow-up activities
● Decorate a large
cardboard box with
string patterns and
cover closely in foil
to make an
impressive chest for
your treasure.
● Draw treasure
maps for your
friends.
● Make your
treasure chest part of
an undersea world
(see page 42).

CHAPTER SIX

Show the children how to create music on their exclusively designed musical instruments, be rulers of all they survey as they parade in their glorious crowns, or explore the world of outer space from the safety and comfort of their very own module.

3D SCULPTURE

Learning objective
To explore shape and form in three dimensions.

Group size
Up to six children.

What you need
Small boxes of various shapes and tubes in a variety of sizes, powder paint, white adhesive, pointed scissors, masking tape.

Setting up
Cut some unusual and interesting holes in the surfaces of a few boxes and tubes and carefully dismantle some others, fitting them back together inside out to give a plain, matt surface.

What to do
Invite the children to each choose a maximum of six 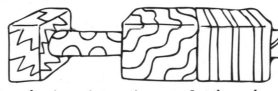 boxes or tubes to join together in an interesting way. Let them choose how to join their boxes – using masking tape eliminates the need to wait for glue to dry but it does not give such a neat finish.

Encourage the children to think before they attach their boxes and to try positioning them in various ways before finally deciding where to fix them. Once the basic structures are complete and are thoroughly dry, invite the children to paint them with fairly thick powder paints (add a little white adhesive to it to prevent excessive flaking when dry).

When all the painted models are completely dry, ask each child to decide which way up their model should be displayed, before gathering the group together to talk about the sculptures.

Questions to ask
Do any of the models look the same as each other? Do any of them contain the same combination of shapes? Are any identically painted? Does any child like one particular model best? Why? Talk about the overall shape of each model. Is it a curvy, rounded sort of sculpture? Or is it angular and sharp? Does it make you want to hold or touch it?

For younger children
Very young children can be very impatient, so be ready to paper-clip or staple their components together to hold them in place until they are taped together more firmly, or until the adhesive dries.

For older children
Encourage them to think about the effect each box or tube will have on the structure – for example, will it cause it to overbalance?

Follow-up activities
● Invite a local sculptor in to demonstrate his (or her) art.
● Make an abstract sculpture from clay, papier mâché or Plasticine.
● Build a huge junk sculpture and paint it with a grey sand and paint mixture to resemble stone.

MUSICAL INSTRUMENTS

Learning objective
To create simple musical instruments with which to explore the world of sound.

Group size
Up to six children.

↑
different
width elastic
bands
↓

What you need
A large selection of junk materials and elastic bands, Sellotape, buttons, rice, thin dowelling.

Setting up
Make a few sample instruments yourself and talk about them with the children before inviting them to use any available materials to create their own instruments.

What to do
Once you start investigating the various items you will probably find that there is no shortage of imaginative ideas. Start with these:
• Make shakers by sticking two yoghurt pots together and placing rice, buttons or pasta inside.
• Tape two different washing-up liquid bottle lids (which often have interesting ridged patterns) together to make a two-tone scraper which can also be tapped with dowelling for further variation.
• Stretch an elastic band lengthwise over a strong tube and pluck the ends, or around a tissue-box and pluck the band where it crosses the open hole.
• Make plastic bottles into shakers by pouring a little sand or gravel inside before sealing. Alternatively, strike them gently with beaters, or tap them with the hand. Some children may manage to produce a sound by blowing across their open tops.
• A marble or small ball sealed inside a coffee tin produces a variety of interesting sounds when tipped, turned, shaken or swirled.

Encourage the children to think about how they will use their instruments and the sorts of sounds they might produce. Allow plenty of time for experimentation with the finished instruments before finally gathering the group together to talk about what they have been doing.

Questions to ask
Invite each child in turn to talk about his instrument. How was it made? What, if anything, is inside it? How is it played? Are there other ways of producing a sound from it? (Let others make suggestions if its creator is unsure.) Is there any way in which the instrument might be improved? (By decorating it in some way.) Would the instrument-maker like to play the group a tune on his instrument?

For younger children
CARE! Ensure that tiny beads and buttons are kept well away from mouths, ears and noses.

For older children
Suggest that they decorate plain instruments – perhaps with old wrapping-paper or sticky-backed plastic.

Follow-up activities
● Use the instruments for rhythm work.
● Listen to each instrument in turn and decide which gives the longest-lasting note.
● Pass an instrument round the group with each child making it produce a different sound.

SOUND MOBILES

Learning objective
To explore the sound-producing qualities of a variety of reclaimed objects.

Group size
Up to six children.

What you need
Wire coat hangers, scraps of bright fabric or crêpe paper, double-sided tape, collection of small hard plastic or metal objects (aluminium pie dishes, milk bottle tops, keys, metal dry-marker pen cases), strong thread, awl, sticky tape, two or three sets of wind chimes.

Setting up
Securely fix a short length of thread (10–20cms) to each small object either with sticky tape or by threading it through a hole made by the awl. Suspend a coat hanger from the ceiling for each child so that it can be worked on at child's eye height. Cover the shoulders of each hanger with double-sided tape, without removing the backing paper.

What to do
Show the children the wind chimes which you have and observe and discuss them together, noticing the comparative lengths of thread and the positions of the various components.

Invite the children to each make their own sound mobile, using a wire coat hanger as a base. Suggest that the mobiles would look more attractive if the hanger was disguised in some way and show everyone how to peel off the backing-strip to reveal the sticky tape to which they can add thin strips of brightly coloured fabrics or paper.

Invite the children to select a number of small objects to tie or tape onto their hangers so that they jangle together to give a pleasant sound. Display your mobiles in a corner near a window which can be opened to provide a gentle breeze.

Questions to ask
What happens if you put the first object at one end of the hanger? (It tips up the other end.)
So where is it best to start? (The centre.) What happens if the objects are too far apart? (They won't touch each other and will make no sound.) What if they are too close? (They won't be able to move properly and might become tangled.) If one end is tipping up, where should the next object go? (At the other end probably.)

For younger children
They may need help to balance their objects evenly along the hanger. Encourage them to put the heavier objects near the centre.

For older children
They may be able to attach their own lengths of thread to the objects.

strong
thread

pierced
hole

pie
dish

double-sided
tape wrapped
around hanger
without
removing
backing
paper

strips of
fabric
folded
over and
stuck
onto
tape

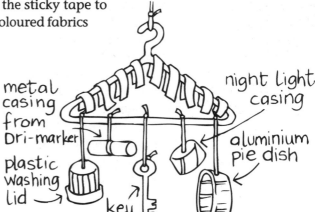

metal
casing
from
Dri-marker

plastic
washing
lid

key

night light
casing

aluminium
pie dish

Follow-up activities
● Learn to play different notes on some real wind instruments.
● Paint pictures of things which rely on the wind to work – windmill, sailing-boat, sailboard or a kite.
● Find out about seeds which are dispersed by the wind.

TEXTURED TEDDY

Learning objective
To explore various soft, textured surfaces.

Group size
Up to six children.

What you need
Photocopiable page 64 for each child, strong white adhesive and brushes, small scraps of soft materials such as cotton wool, wool, fur, corduroy, suede, felt or velvet, scissors, card or stiff paper.

Setting up
Talk about teddies and how they are generally warm, soft and cuddly.

What to do
Tell the children they are going to make a teddy picture using some soft materials. Show the different materials which you have and invite the children to feel them all and to decide which one they would like to use. Explain that they must use only one fabric type for the whole teddy so that it looks attractive as well as feeling good. Encourage them to stroke the materials in both directions and with fingers, hands, backs of hands and to feel them against their faces to help them decide.

Once the children have all decided, hand out the photocopiable sheet and invite them to cover the teddy closely with their chosen fabric, trying to leave no spaces and to stay within the outline. (Black felt features can always be added later if the children find it difficult to avoid covering these.) As the children work, talk to them about what they are doing and encourage them to describe how the feel of the material might be changing as it comes into contact with the adhesive.

When the teddies are thoroughly dry they can be cut out and remounted onto card for a really neat finish.

Questions to ask
Why is it important to leave no spaces on your teddy? (Because then it would not feel the same all over.) Why should you try not to use too much glue? (Because it will take a very long time to dry and it might make the material go hard.) What happens if your fingers get too sticky? (Bits of fabric get stuck to them – especially cotton wool, wool and felt.) So what should you do about this? (Wash your hands before continuing your work.)

For younger children
Enlarge the photocopiable sheet to A3 size.

For older children
Encourage them to make a frame for their remounted teddy.

Follow-up activities
● Close your eyes and feel the differently textured teddies. Can you tell which is which?
● Make some teddy-shaped biscuits.
● Make a display of famous bear characters like Winnie-the-Pooh, Rupert Bear and Paddington, and read some of their stories.
● Colour in the photocopiable teddy and add a fabric waistcoat or bow-tie.

CROWNS AND TIARAS

Learning objective
To make and use some regal headgear.

Group size
Up to six children.

What you need
Paper or card, scissors, adhesive, sequins, sweet wrappers or off-cuts of Cellophane and foil, glitter, felt-tipped pens.

What to do
Invite the children to make a tiara or crown.
Crown: fold a piece of paper (30cms by 20cms) in half lengthwise. Draw parallel lines, about 3cms apart, from the folded edge to within 3cms of the open edge. Keeping the paper folded, cut along each parallel line, taking care not to go beyond its end. Carefully unfold the cut paper and lay it flat with the raised crease down on the table. Decorate the crown using felt-tipped pens, scraps of Cellophane, glitter or foil. Finally, glue along one long edge and gently fold the other edge down on top of it without making a crease, thus making a decorated 'lamb-chop' frill. Adjust to fit before securing with adhesive or Sellotape.
Tiara: fold a piece of paper (30cms by 10cms) in half from left to right. Draw a simple line from the folded edge, tapering down to about 3cms, and a further design on the folded edge that will be cut away later to make a central hole. Keeping the paper folded, cut along the lines. Unfold to reveal a shaped band with a central cut-away design. Glue a sweet wrapper behind the hole to give a neat finish to the inset 'jewel' and decorate the tiara.

As the children work remind them that the headgear is for people who need to look very grand, so they must be very neat and precise in their work. When the crowns and tiaras are dry, invite the children to put them on, and practise walking and moving regally.

Questions to ask
What are real crowns made of? (Gold, silver, precious jewels.) What might happen if you moved too quickly or tipped your head about too much? (The crown might fall off.) How might you feel to be a king or queen during an important procession? (Important, proud, grand, nervous, scared.) What sort of clothes might you wear with your crown? (Robes, cloaks, gowns or suits made of velvet, silk, fur or brocade.)

For younger children
Help by drawing the initial designs on the folded paper for younger children.

For older children
Show them how to fold their tiaras to create more complex cut-out designs.

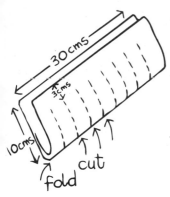
30cms
3cms
10cms
cut
fold

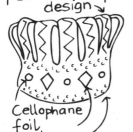
felt-tipped pen design
Cellophane
foil
glitter
fold

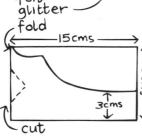
15cms
10cms
3cms
cut

Cellophane window
sequins
foil
felt-tipped
pen design glitter

Follow-up activities
● Make a collection of story books featuring royal characters.
● Wearing the crowns (and cloaks made from old curtains), parade to the sound of majestic music – bowing and curtseying elegantly.
● Compare the feel of different fabrics.

JACK FROST

Learning objective
To create a collage
using different
materials to express
the cold.

Group size
Up to six children.

What you need
Scraps of white, grey, silver and pale blue materials such
as Cellophane, wool, paper, foil, florists' ribbon, glitter,
adhesive, scissors, pinking shears, a sheet of black paper
(as large as possible), chalk or white crayon, wintry
pictures featuring frost and ice.

Setting up
Look at the pictures of wintry scenes which you have
available and talk to the children about what they notice,
paying particular attention to colour and general
appearance of the frost and ice. Mention icicles and
discuss their shape. Using the chalk, draw a large,
prancing stick person on the black paper.

What to do
Invite the children to cover the stick person with ice-coloured shapes
to make Jack Frost. If you have sufficient wall space available at a
convenient working height, this is an ideal opportunity to let the
children experience working vertically rather than on a horizontal
surface.

Suggest that they might use pinking shears or cut the materials
into long, thin triangles for a really spiky effect. Encourage them to
leave the points of the triangles unstuck so that they will curl and
stick out from the paper, and to overlap shapes to fill all the spaces
on Jack Frost's body. Use glitter to fill any small gaps.

Leave the picture to dry thoroughly before drawing the group
together to view and discuss it. Encourage the
children to gently touch the collage – with
fingers, palms and backs of hands.

Questions to ask
What does our Jack Frost picture look like?
(Sparkly, white, silver, shiny, blue.) Is that like
real frost? (Yes.) What does the collage feel like?
(Prickly, spiky, rough.) What does real frost feel
like? (Cold, rough, spiky.) How does it make you
feel when you look at Jack Frost? (Cold and
shivery!) Feel different materials on the picture.

For younger children
Supply ready-cut materials if necessary.

For older children
Encourage older children to select suitable
materials themselves from a wide range of
colours and types.

Follow-up activities
● Undertake some
explorative play with
a water-tray full of
ice-cubes.
● Experiment with
different materials
like salt, sugar and
soap flakes to make
little collage
snowmen.
● Paint a picture
using reds, oranges
and yellows and
another using blues,
greys and greens and
compare how they
make you feel.
● Go outside on a
frosty day and look
for cobwebs, frozen
puddles and frosty
patterns on windows
or cars.

GIANT HEADS

Learning objective
To experience working
with papier mâché

Group size
Up to four children.

What you need
Balloons, balloon pump, petroleum jelly, newspapers, white newsprint
or kitchen paper, cardboard egg cartons, paste, paint and brushes,
bowl of water, wool, round margarine tubs, scissors, adhesive.

Setting up
Cut egg cartons into single sections. Cut the newspapers into 2cms
wide strips for the children. Inflate a balloon for each child. CARE!
Make sure an adult blows up the balloons using the balloon pump,
warn the children about popping them and be aware that some
children may be distressed if this happens.

What to do
Tell the children you are going to make some giant heads by covering
balloons in paper and paste. Explain that this will take a very long
time and that it has to be done in different stages. Give each child a
balloon and invite them to coat their balloons in petroleum jelly and
to place it on a margarine tub to steady it. Show them how to pick up
one strip of newspaper, dip it in water and wrap it around the balloon,
repeating the process until the entire balloon is covered. Next,
demonstrate how to paste strips of paper and again cover the entire
balloon. Repeat until there are at least four layers of paper (alternately
wet and pasted) covering the balloon.

Leave to dry thoroughly for about a week – or until firm to the
touch. Burst and remove the balloon. Show the children how to glue
an egg carton nose into position and apply one coat of glued strips of
white paper over the entire head – including the nose. Leave to dry
overnight.

Let the children paint their 'heads' all over in flesh tones and again
leave them to dry before finally adding facial features and wool hair.
Talk to the children throughout the various stages, encouraging them
to notice changes in the look and feel of the paper as they work.

Questions to ask
What does the wet paper feel like? (Cold, wet, slippery, soft.) What
happens if you handle it roughly? (It tears!) What does the gluey
paper feel like? (Slimey, sticky, smooth, cold.) What happens to your
hands after a while? (They get cold, wet, sticky and covered in ink.)
Why must we cover the whole balloon with paper? (Otherwise there
will be holes in the finished head.)

For younger children
Let them use alternate layers of newspaper and white paper to help
them see where they are up to when covering the balloon.

For older children
Encourage them to add details such as eyebrows, ears and eyelashes.

coating of petroleum jelly

margarine tub
newspaper strips

wool hair
painted features
egg carton nose

Follow-up activities
● Stuff some old
clothes with
newspaper to give
your head a body.
● Use your head as a
ventriloquist's
dummy.
● Make a list of
words that rhyme
with 'head'.

SPACESHIP

Learning objective
To create an
imaginative role-play
environment.

Group size
Whole group for initial
planning, up to six
children for practical
activities.

What you need
Books and pictures about space, junk materials such as black fabric, black, white, silver and holographic paper, large cardboard boxes and tubes, plastic lemonade bottles, pencil, scissors, adhesive, double-sided tape. Disposable boiler suits, white gloves and socks, toy tool-kit and *Blackboard Bear* by Martha Alexander (Walker Books) are useful though not essential.

Setting up
Talk about space. Read *Blackboard Bear* and suggest that the group might create a spaceship. Decide upon a suitable area for it and spend some time recording ideas and suggestions for the design.

What to do
Invite the children to play a major part in preparing the area by making as many of the props as possible themselves. This will take several sessions, but it will also give the group a sense of ownership and therefore encourage them to take care of the finished environment. Try to give every child the opportunity to help in some way.

Cover the walls with black paper and enclose the area with a black fabric screen or curtain. Place two large cardboard boxes (about 75cm high) against one wall and decorate them to represent control panels. Add a paper frame for the cockpit windscreen and cover the walls with planets, stars, moons and spacecraft.

If possible provide a few disposable boiler-suits that have been cut down to size, make some cylindrical cardboard helmets covered in foil and add coiled paper umbilical cords to attach to astronauts leaving the confines of the spaceship. Make oxygen tanks by covering lemonade bottles in white paper. Use double-sided tape to attach fabric straps to buckle round the waist. Have a tool-kit handy if possible for repair jobs in and outside the ship, and white gloves and socks for total protection.

Questions to ask
Why do astronauts need umbilical cords? (So they don't float into space.) Why do they need helmets and oxygen tanks? (Because there is no air to breathe in space.) What sort of things might be seen from spacecraft windows? (Planets, stars, satellites.) What do you think it would be like to visit the moon?

For younger children
Make star-cutting simpler by using two overlaid equilateral triangles.

For older children
Encourage them to draw their own plans for the area.

Follow-up activities
● Practise counting backwards from 10.
● Listen to parts of *The Planet Suite* by Gustav Holst.
● Paint pictures of an alien from an unknown planet.
● Use papier mâché to make a lunar landscape for small world play.

PHOTOCOPIABLES

Name _____

Name _____

Match the houses with the same shapes.

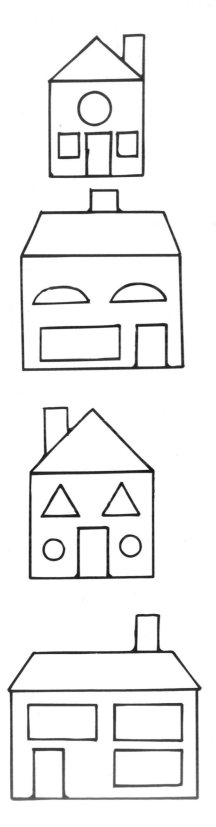

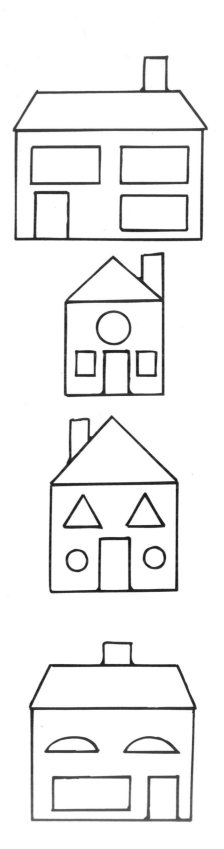

Name _____

Write names on the envelopes.

Name _____

Cut out both wheels. Pierce a hole in the centre of each. Place wheel A on top of wheel B and join with a paper fastener. For a sturdier wheel, glue to thin card before assembling.

A.

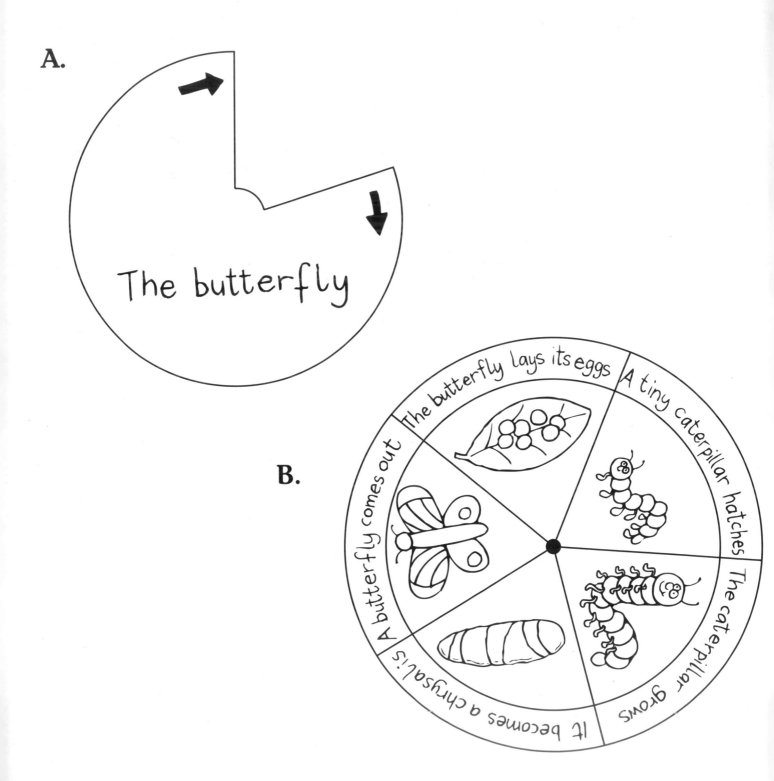

The butterfly

B.

The butterfly lays its eggs

A tiny caterpillar hatches

The caterpillar grows

It becomes a chrysalis

A butterfly comes out

Name _____

Colour the correct number of skittles on each line.

3

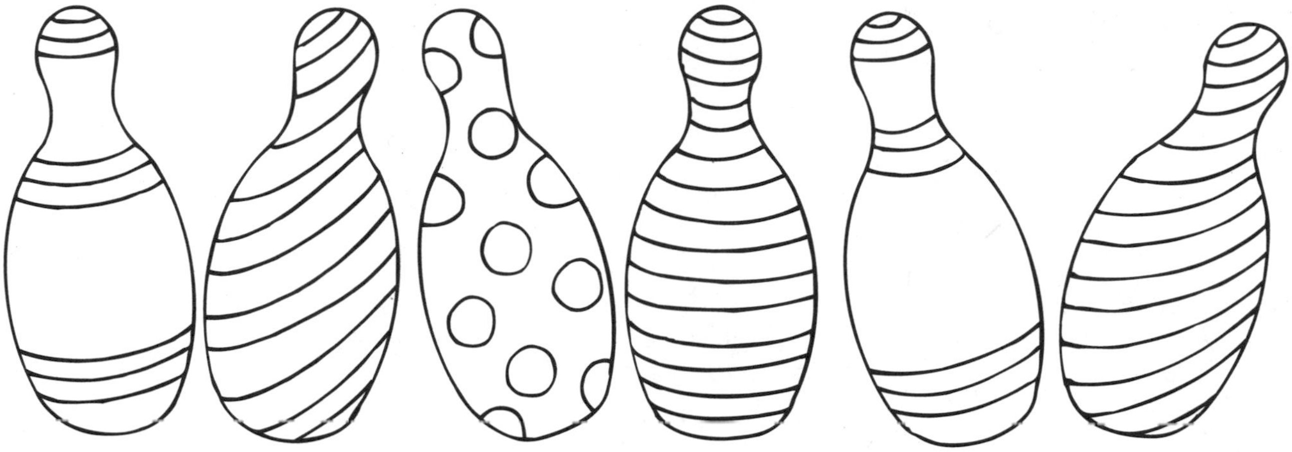

5

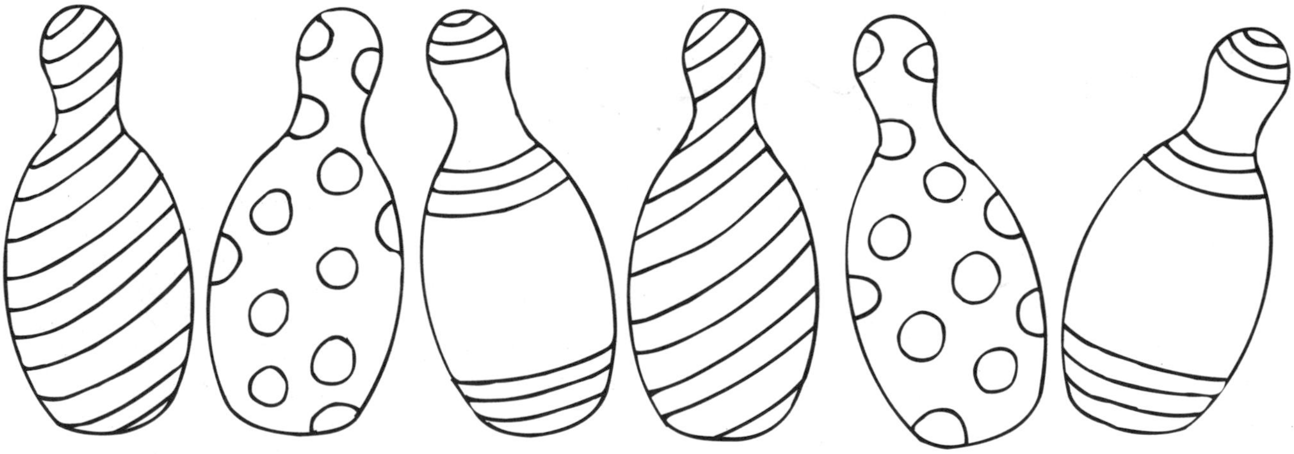

2

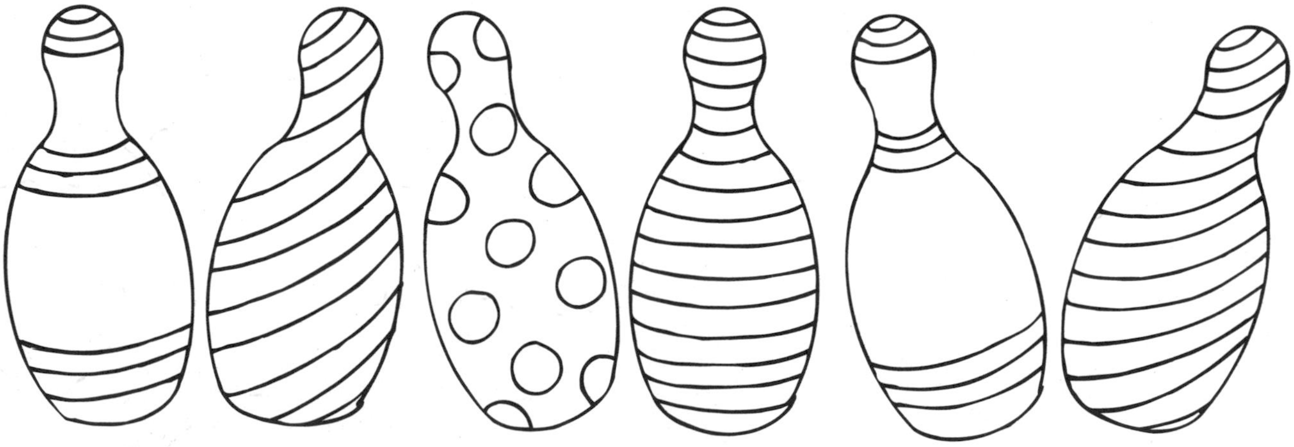

Name _____